FRANCIS FRITH'S

PETERSFIELD - A HIS
CELEBRATION

THE FRANCIS FRITH COLLECTION

www.francisfrith.com

PETERSFIELD

A HISTORY & CELEBRATION

KENNETH HICK

THE FRANCIS FRITH COLLECTION

www.francisfrith.com

First published in the United Kingdom in 2005
by The Francis Frith Collection®

Hardback Edition 2005 ISBN 1-84589-214-3
Paperback Edition 2011 ISBN 978-1-84589-598-3

British Library Cataloguing in Publication Data

Petersfield - A History & Celebration
Kenneth Hick

The Francis Frith Collection
Oakley Business Park, Wylye Road,
Dinton, Wiltshire SP3 5EU
Tel: +44 (0) 1722 716 376
Email: info@francisfrith.co.uk
www.francisfrith.com

Printed and bound in England

Front Cover: **PETERSFIELD, MARKET SQUARE c1955** P48008t

Additional modern photographs by Kenneth Hick.

Domesday extract used in timeline by kind permission of
Alecto Historical Editions, www.domesdaybook.org
Aerial photographs reproduced under licence from
Simmons Aerofilms Limited.
Historical Ordnance Survey maps reproduced under licence from
Homecheck.co.uk

CONTENTS

PETERSFIELD
A HISTORY & CELEBRATION

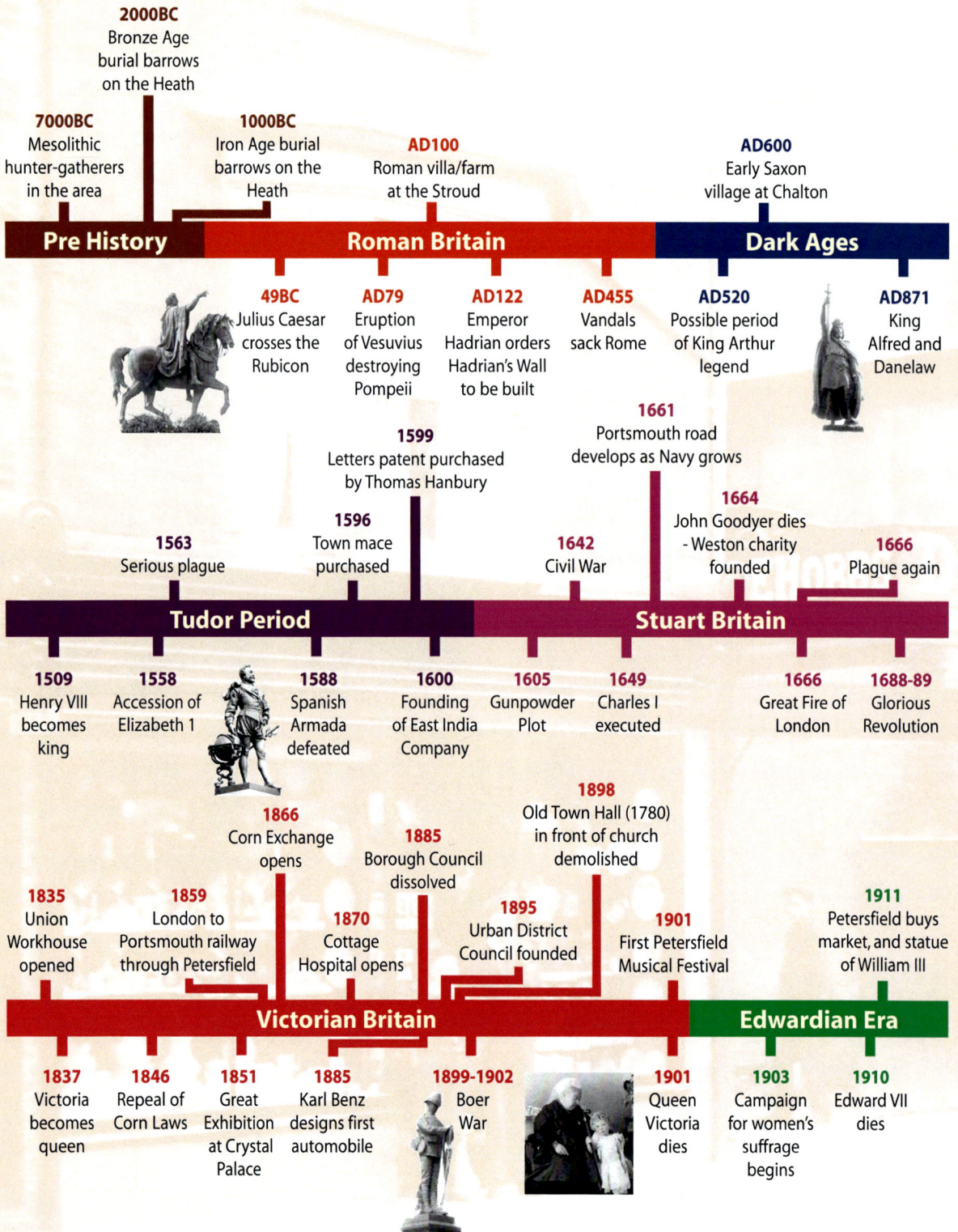

2000BC
Bronze Age burial barrows on the Heath

7000BC
Mesolithic hunter-gatherers in the area

1000BC
Iron Age burial barrows on the Heath

AD100
Roman villa/farm at the Stroud

AD600
Early Saxon village at Chalton

Pre History | Roman Britain | Dark Ages

49BC
Julius Caesar crosses the Rubicon

AD79
Eruption of Vesuvius destroying Pompeii

AD122
Emperor Hadrian orders Hadrian's Wall to be built

AD455
Vandals sack Rome

AD520
Possible period of King Arthur legend

AD871
King Alfred and Danelaw

1661
Portsmouth road develops as Navy grows

1599
Letters patent purchased by Thomas Hanbury

1664
John Goodyer dies - Weston charity founded

1596
Town mace purchased

1666
Plague again

1563
Serious plague

1642
Civil War

Tudor Period | Stuart Britain

1509
Henry VIII becomes king

1558
Accession of Elizabeth 1

1588
Spanish Armada defeated

1600
Founding of East India Company

1605
Gunpowder Plot

1649
Charles I executed

1666
Great Fire of London

1688-89
Glorious Revolution

1898
Old Town Hall (1780) in front of church demolished

1866
Corn Exchange opens

1885
Borough Council dissolved

1911
Petersfield buys market, and statue of William III

1835
Union Workhouse opened

1859
London to Portsmouth railway through Petersfield

1870
Cottage Hospital opens

1895
Urban District Council founded

1901
First Petersfield Musical Festival

Victorian Britain | Edwardian Era

1837
Victoria becomes queen

1846
Repeal of Corn Laws

1851
Great Exhibition at Crystal Palace

1885
Karl Benz designs first automobile

1899-1902
Boer War

1901
Queen Victoria dies

1903
Campaign for women's suffrage begins

1910
Edward VII dies

HISTORICAL TIMELINE FOR PETERSFIELD

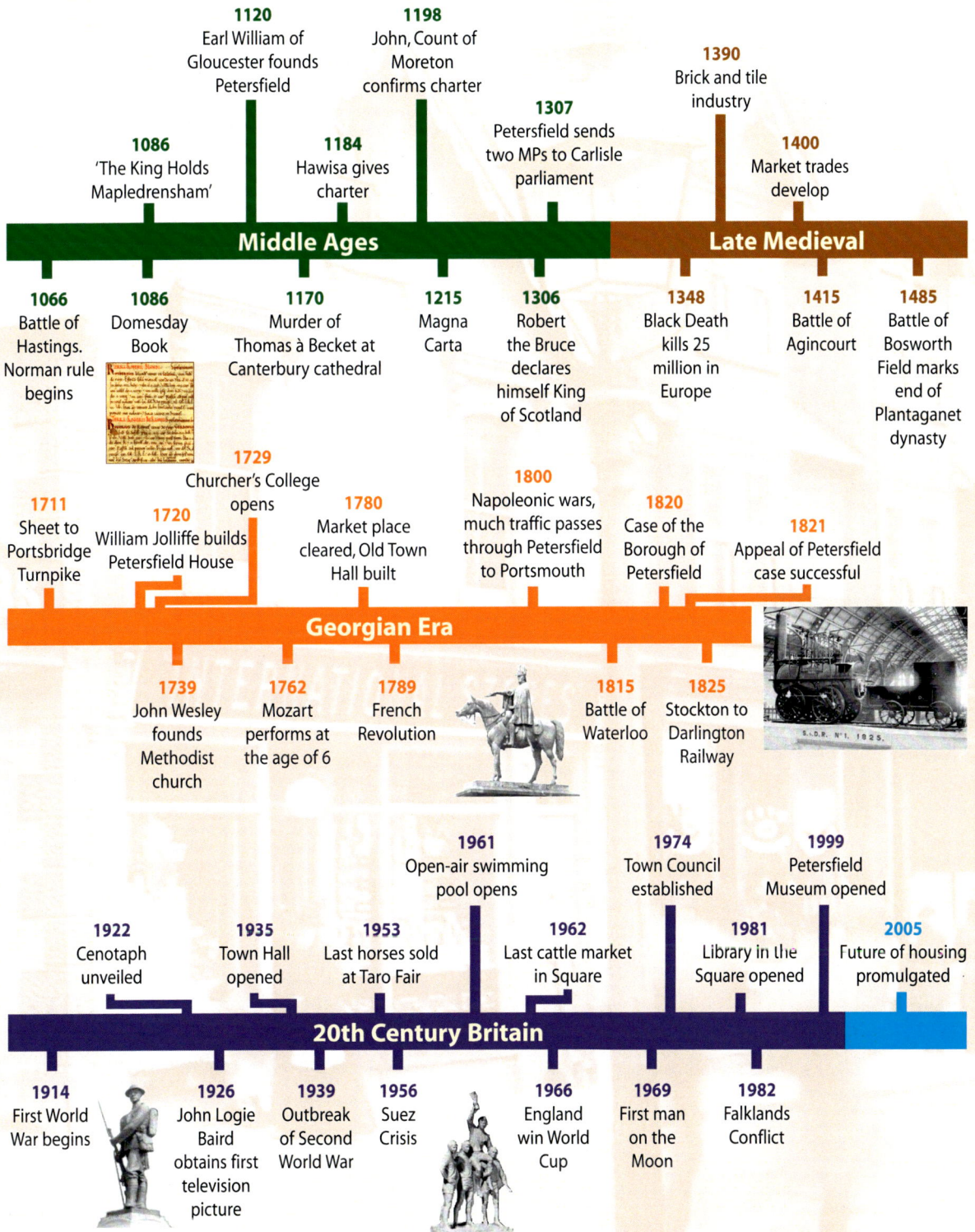

Middle Ages | Late Medieval

1120 Earl William of Gloucester founds Petersfield

1198 John, Count of Moreton confirms charter

1390 Brick and tile industry

1086 'The King Holds Mapledrensham'

1184 Hawisa gives charter

1307 Petersfield sends two MPs to Carlisle parliament

1400 Market trades develop

1066 Battle of Hastings. Norman rule begins

1086 Domesday Book

1170 Murder of Thomas à Becket at Canterbury cathedral

1215 Magna Carta

1306 Robert the Bruce declares himself King of Scotland

1348 Black Death kills 25 million in Europe

1415 Battle of Agincourt

1485 Battle of Bosworth Field marks end of Plantaganet dynasty

Georgian Era

1729 Churcher's College opens

1780 Market place cleared, Old Town Hall built

1800 Napoleonic wars, much traffic passes through Petersfield to Portsmouth

1820 Case of the Borough of Petersfield

1711 Sheet to Portsbridge Turnpike

1720 William Jolliffe builds Petersfield House

1821 Appeal of Petersfield case successful

1739 John Wesley founds Methodist church

1762 Mozart performs at the age of 6

1789 French Revolution

1815 Battle of Waterloo

1825 Stockton to Darlington Railway

20th Century Britain

1961 Open-air swimming pool opens

1974 Town Council established

1999 Petersfield Museum opened

1922 Cenotaph unveiled

1935 Town Hall opened

1953 Last horses sold at Taro Fair

1962 Last cattle market in Square

1981 Library in the Square opened

2005 Future of housing promulgated

1914 First World War begins

1926 John Logie Baird obtains first television picture

1939 Outbreak of Second World War

1956 Suez Crisis

1966 England win World Cup

1969 First man on the Moon

1982 Falklands Conflict

CHAPTER ONE

FOUNDATIONS

MOST OF this first chapter has to be supposition, for the facts are few and far between, but certainly two requirements were just as important in the past as they are now in the 21st century: firstly, the lie of the land was and is still critical to a successful place to camp for the night; and secondly, man's intelligence was and is needed to make the right decisions on where to camp. Man's knowledge may be way above that of Stone Age man, but his intelligence is no higher than that of the first-class innovators who built the pyramids or Stonehenge.

Take a bird's eye view of the western end of the Weald. Here there is the junction between the thin line of upper greensand and the South Downs chalk. These features, combined with the presence of the River Rother, form the basis of a place for prehistoric hunter-gatherers to halt awhile and shelter during their wanderings looking for food.

It must be realised that the surrounding dense woodlands that covered the area for miles around would be hard to navigate. It might be easy to follow the tracks left by animals, but how would the Stone Age people find the way back to their starting point, past the many junctions and turnings not noticed during their outward journey? On the other hand, a journey in a canoe dug out from the trunk of a tree would mean few, if any, possibilities for losing the way, and the River Rother provided just such a

FLINT TOOLS FOUND ON THE HEATH 2005 ZZZ04804 (Petersfield Museum)

way through the Sussex forest and up to Sheet.

Stone Age people would have found it easier to walk up to the ridge in the direction of the present Durford Road. The ground there is sandy, and the trees not so big and thick. Turning westwards towards the setting sun, they would have found a marsh, rich with birds and animals to catch for food and with water to drink. They would realise that they could camp there and avoid getting flooded out by the river every now and then. That marshy area was the present Heath Pond. It is pure conjecture that Stone Age people camped here, but it is highly likely. This was Stone

Fact File

The way to see something of what Petersfield Heath used to look like is to go right across the county to Breamore, near Fordingbridge, and look at the marsh there: you can see a little stream, a marshy pond, and grazing cattle, even geese. Today both of these areas have cricket fields; at Breamore there is still a thatched cricket pavilion.

Age Petersfield. During that time, flint tools were left behind on the heath and just to the south-west of Westmark, on the eastern edge of Sheet.

A TUMULUS 2005 ZZZ04805 (Kenneth Hick)

And now to the greatest mystery: who were the people who raised the tumuli or burial mounds on Petersfield Heath during the Bronze Age some 1,000 years after the Stone Age? Today, Petersfield is home to one of the most numerous collections of Bronze Age burial mounds in England. Unfortunately, the planting of conifers on the mounds in Victorian times and the mixed tree growth of the last 50 years has successfully camouflaged the outline of the tumuli and largely hidden them from the casual view (see page 11). To create mounds like this would have required the labour of many people, and they appear to have been built over many years, if not centuries. So where did these people live? Why have they left us no clues to tell us where they came from?

Did they come from miles around to bury the ashes of their dead princes here? Were they nomads carrying the remains from a fair distance to a sacred spot or a clearing in the forest? Or is it possible that someone may yet find their habitation site here within the town itself? In all probability we shall never ever know the answer, and the mystery will remain for all time.

THE POND c1955 P48034

There are a total of 21 barrows on Petersfield Heath, and there are examples of the four basic types of barrow: bowl, disc, saucer and bell. Sir Stuart Piggott, the eminent archaeologist, was educated at Churcher's College; he became fascinated by the heath and its barrows, which set him on his chosen career. Some have even called the heath a Bronze/Iron Age Westminster Abbey.

Petersfield is very lucky in having Butser Ancient Farm close at hand. Here many fascinating discoveries have been made about life in pre-Roman Britain. The remains of Iron Age farm animals have been studied, and their nearest surviving equivalents identified; where possible, live examples of these animals can be seen at the farm. More spectacular are the recreated buildings - they display the inventiveness of our predecessors.

The great roundhouse was built using information derived from the excavation that took place on Cowdown at Longbridge Deverel in Wiltshire. The excavation gave positive clues about the construction of the building, and the archaeologists re-created it from the logical interpretation of that information. There is every reason to believe that any similar Iron Age building in the vicinity of Petersfield would exhibit much the same features.

BUTSER ANCIENT FARM, THE GREAT ROUNDHOUSE 2005 P48738k
(Kenneth Hick, reproduced by courtesy of Butser Ancient Farm)

After the invasion of the Roman armies under Claudius in AD 43, Celtic tribal barriers became blurred, and Petersfield was bypassed by the Roman lines of communication. Chichester was the local focus of the occupation, and no road from Chichester came closer than Iping, some eight miles away. Nevertheless, a Roman farmstead was built at the Stroud ('stroud' means an area of brambles and stunted trees on marshy ground) beside an east-west track that can still be discerned as a public footpath.

STROUD ROMAN FARM/VILLA

Excavated in 1908, the villa, or more correctly, farm, was built immediately to the north of the track leading from Winchester to Sussex at the Stroud to the west of Petersfield. It was a brick and timber construction, with farm and bath-house buildings arranged around a courtyard. It is interesting that the house, rectangular in plan, had two parallel rows of pillars which gave support to the roof in the style of a Roman basilica. The excavation was carried out by pupils of Bedales School under the direction of a teacher, Moray Williams. Note the drainage channels visible in the photograph.

THE REMAINS OF THE ROMAN VILLA 1908 ZZZ04807 (Petersfield Museum)

During the next 600 years there is no sign of anything happening at all in the area. It must be that a very basic existence was eked out by Anglo-Saxon farmers where Petersfield now stands. There would be tracks to the nearby villages, and the route of these would vary according to the weather conditions and the consequent mud, or lack of mud, on them. One track would certainly have been the Winchester to Sussex track going west

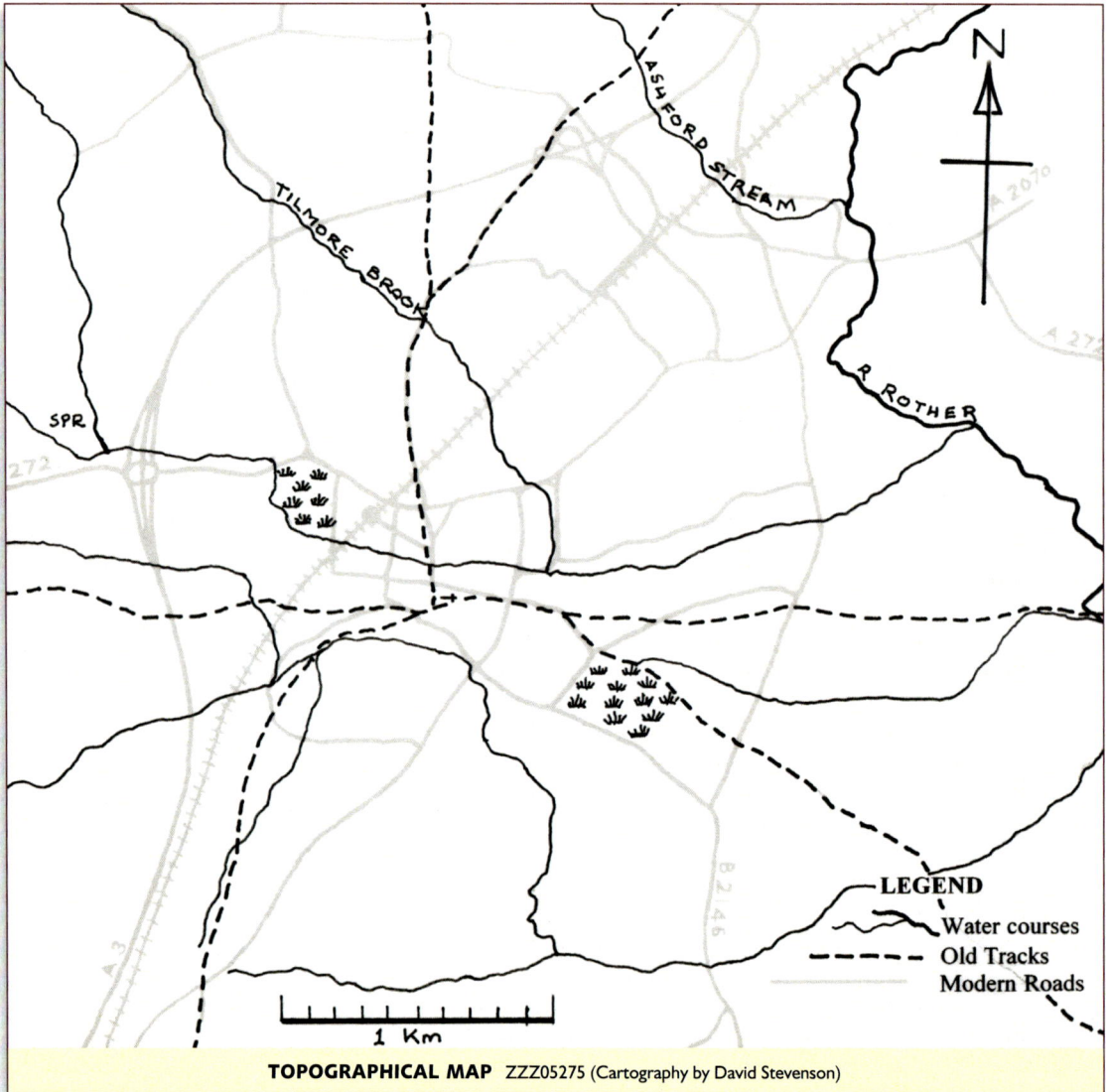

TOPOGRAPHICAL MAP ZZZ05275 (Cartography by David Stevenson)

This map shows the streams and tracks that formed the focus on which Petersfield was founded, superimposed on the present-day road and rail patterns. The position of today's Square can be discerned where the tracks converge and the streams are close together.

to east and avoiding the marshes at Potter's Flood (Frenchman's Road), Borough Road, Tilmore Valley, and the south-east of the present heath.

It would be reasonable to assume, from clues left behind, that this track would take the route of the railway footbridge by what is now Travis Perkins, straight along the Borough to The Spain, up Sheep Street, along the sandy ridge on which the High Street is built, straight to the north of the Heath and across to Durford Road; then over the River Rother into what is now Sussex at Durford Abbey.

From the earliest times there would most probably be trade with the coast in imported goods, fish, salt and other commodities; the nearest coast was at Warblington or at Emsworth. The direct way to Petersfield would be through Rowlands Castle, to Finchdean and onwards to Buriton, along the track to Bolinge Hill. Then the route would lead across the low-lying land to Landpits, and into the town at The Spain, where it probably met the track from Winchester.

So there was a fairly important crossroads here, with its attendant excuse for a stop for refreshment and possibly an exchange of goods and information. There is a likelihood that another track would wend its way up over Tilmore Hill, past the site of today's Harrow Inn and on to the village that we now call West Liss. We must remember that all these routes would have been developed well before the Norman invasion, and could well have been established over the previous 1,500 years; things only moved at a snail's pace in those far-off days.

THE SPAIN c1955 P48014

CHAPTER TWO

OUT OF THE GROUND

A HISTORY & CELEBRATION

IN THIS CHAPTER I want to introduce into this narrative the wool and leather trade, and cover the tremendous growth that occurred during the period covered by medieval times and the Tudor, Stuart and Georgian eras. I will also tell the story of the controversial Baroness Petersfield!

1066 is the date that every Englishman remembers; it firmly fixes in our minds the halfway point between the present day and the birth of Jesus. William the Conqueror landed in East Sussex, and his Norman knights quickly established themselves in the south of England. They consolidated their power and subjugated the Anglo-Saxons, assisted by the construction of motte and bailey castles (these had surrounding defences with a fortification of either stone or wood, with an earth mound inside them). The nearest castle to Petersfield is at Privett, just south of Bailey Green, and there is another in West Sussex at Verdley Wood, close to the present day Midhurst television transmitter. They were built where the surrounding area, for perhaps 20 miles around, could be kept under surveillance during the conquest of the country, and not necessarily in centres of population.

But of course the crowning event of the Norman Conquest was the great stock-taking that led to the creation of the Domesday Book. Search high and low, but you will not find a mention of Petersfield in the whole book; the only conclusion that can drawn from this is that there was no such place as Petersfield in 1086 when the book was collated. The Domesday Book does, however, include

details of Mapledrensham (also known as Mapledurham): 'The King holds the Manor of Mapledrensham in demesne, and it was held by Ulveve, and in the possession of Queen Matilda'.

Mapledrensham is the present day Buriton. But in 1086 Buriton included Sheet and Petersfield; it was indeed fairly large. It was from Buriton that people came to work in the fields to the north of the village, and they would very likely break off from their labours to attend prayers at a chapel of rest dedicated to St Peter in the Fields (Petersfield). It was to be another 34 years before Petersfield came into being and was granted a charter.

Within 54 years of the Norman landing and the Battle of Hastings, Earl William of Gloucester had the idea of founding a town at the crossroads by the chapel in the fields. He worked out that he could add to the value of his holdings in much the same way as towns today create industrial estates to enhance their revenues.

That he granted a charter to his infant town cannot be denied, but its existence in 1184 after the civil wars of King Steven was so much in doubt that his widow, Hawisa, granted a renewal of the charter, which still exists. This charter granted the town's burgesses 'all liberties and free customs which the citizens of Winchester who are in a Merchants Guild have in their city and let them have the same in a Guild of Merchants as my husband, William, Earl of Gloucester, granted them by this charter'. Some have drawn the conclusion that Petersfield was the equivalent in status to Winchester, but I think it more likely that Winchester was being held up to the country as a model of local government for emulation. This model would be copied by others seeking to adopt what today is termed best custom and practice. Hawisa's charter was confirmed by a further grant by John, Count of Moreton (Mortain), who then lived at nearby East Meon. This 1198 confirmation was made one year before he was to become famous as King John, the king who lost his jewels in the Wash. Both charters are owned by Petersfield Town Council and held in the County Record Office at Winchester.

Sheep could be said to have been the basis for the economy of the town for many years. It was the sheep that had denuded the downs of what scrub they had and turned them into a sheep's paradise. They were slaughtered for the dining tables of the well-to-do. Later the valleys were cleared of forest, and cattle, which also provided meat for the trenchers and plates of the wealthy, were grazed on the resulting fields. Where there was slaughtering of these animals, there followed the manufacture of wool and of leather. And so Petersfield's first industrial estate came into being.

The cattle hides would first be placed in curing pits full of tanning liquid; this was water to which small pieces of oak bark had been added, thereby producing a mild form of tannic acid. The skins then had to be neutralised by the use of lime. The skins of the sheep were treated differently in that they produced blankets for beds in the cold of winter or were shorn to make delicate sheepskin gloves.

Petersfield was famous for the manufacture of woollen cloth called kersey. After the wool

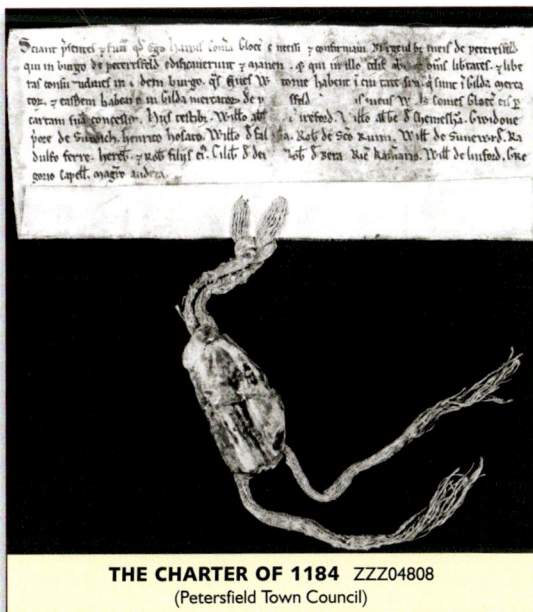

THE CHARTER OF 1184 ZZZ04808
(Petersfield Town Council)

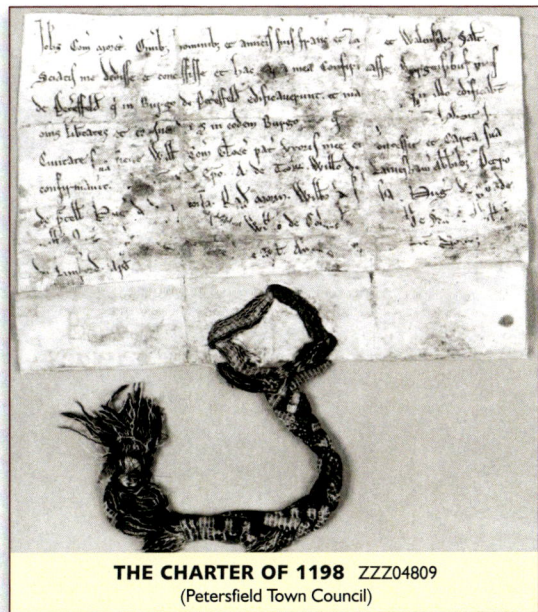

THE CHARTER OF 1198 ZZZ04809
(Petersfield Town Council)

had been fulled, carded and spun, long yarns were woven into a coarse ribbed cloth and this was called kersey. It was very popular in London, where some merchants from the town were prosecuted for selling substandard bolts of the cloth. (The name kersey has no known connection with Kersey, the town in Suffolk).

Wool was produced by summer shearing of the sheep. Before being spun into wool, the thick oily lanolin would have to be extracted from the fleece. The process was

A POUNDING, OR FULLING, MILL

A thick pounding board was lowered onto the wool and fuller's earth and a long arm attached. Half way along the arm was a pivot, and the other end, complete with paddle, was placed into the stream of water which would push the paddle down until the position could not be maintained. Down came the pounding board and thumped the contents of the mixture so that the lanolin was released by the wool and absorbed by the fuller's earth. This could go on for between two days and a week. The process would not require a great head of water; the south stream would meet all Petersfield's needs.

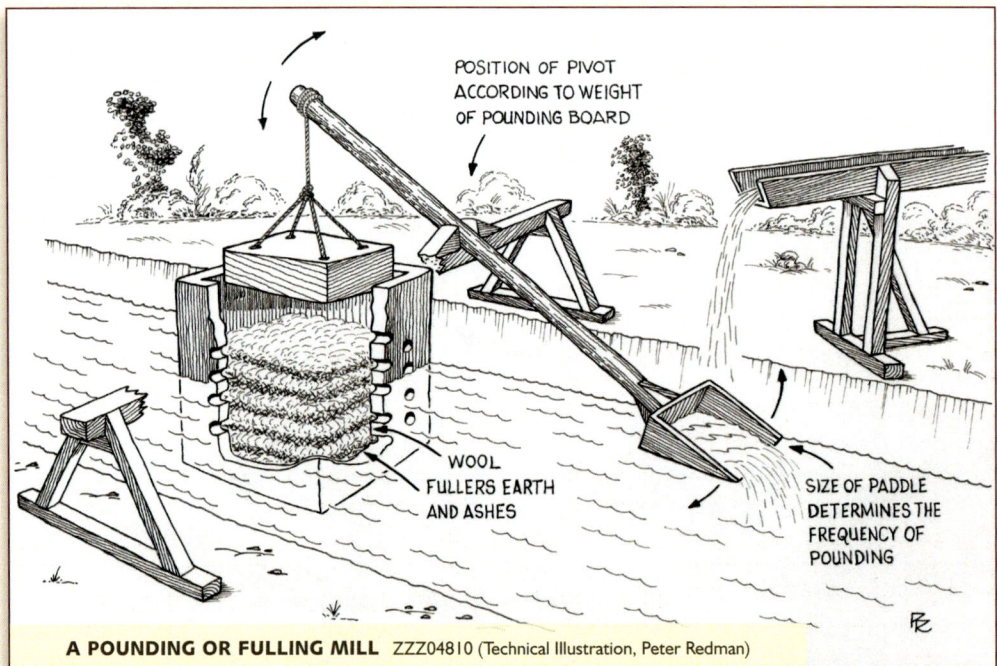

POSITION OF PIVOT
ACCORDING TO WEIGHT
OF POUNDING BOARD

WOOL
FULLERS EARTH
AND ASHES

SIZE OF PADDLE
DETERMINES THE
FREQUENCY OF
POUNDING

A POUNDING OR FULLING MILL ZZZ04810 (Technical Illustration, Peter Redman)

called fulling; it was carried out in a pit into which fuller's earth, and possibly ashes, would be interlayered with the wool, and the pit then flooded with water. Sometimes this arrangement is referred to as a 'pounding mill'. At the end of the 13th century these mills were referred to as ' instruments of a veritable industrial revolution'.

The site of all this activity was in an area on the edge of the town and by the south stream, the present site of Tesco's car-park, but no signs of this hive of medieval industry remain. The reason is that William Jolliffe decided that he wanted the area cleared away from the front of his new 1720 house and an ambitious water garden substituted.

The house only lasted some 73 years - it was demolished in 1793.

Let us return to the founding of Petersfield. The positioning of a new town would be important. The Square and the High Street are strategically placed on slightly higher ground between the two streams that flow eastwards away from the town. They would take away all the town's unwanted rubbish and sewage, and bring in fresh water from the higher ground to the west. Many of the springs issue from below the escarpment at Steep, where the impermeable clay overlies loamy soils. In the town the lie of the land is downwards from the High Street and the Square towards the streams (with the slope to the north stream

THE SITE OF THE TANYARDS, TESCO CAR PARK 2005 P48722k (Kenneth Hick)

not so sharp), which kept the main parts of the town free from flooding.

The town would then have become a centre for tradespeople of all persuasions. Some of the trades have vanished into antiquity, while others are very recognisable, even after 700 years. Cooks, butchers, carpenters, thatchers, wheelwrights, carriers, cordwainers, bakers, coopers, basket makers, rope makers, roofers and so on would be well established in a town such as Petersfield. People from a large surrounding area would then, as now, be talking about the town as the place to go to if something a bit 'special' were needed.

People would walk down the High Street and know every inch of it, just as we still do today. Babies would be born and grow up into young men and women who would

be married in St Peter's Church. After a life of labour, the hard-working townsfolk would be laid to rest in the church's burial ground. But of all this we have very little knowledge; much of the history up to and after the Norman Conquest is the subject of speculation.

Perhaps it would be as well at this point to give an example of the relationship between the conquering Normans and the Anglo-Saxons whom they held in servitude. The serfs or villeins gave their own Anglo-Saxon names to the animals they looked after, pigs, cows, and sheep. On the other hand, the cultivated Norman lords, who were the people who ate the meat from the animals, referred to pork, beef and mutton, all with a basis in the language of France.

HIGH STREET c1965 P48043

ST PETER'S CHURCH c1955 48036

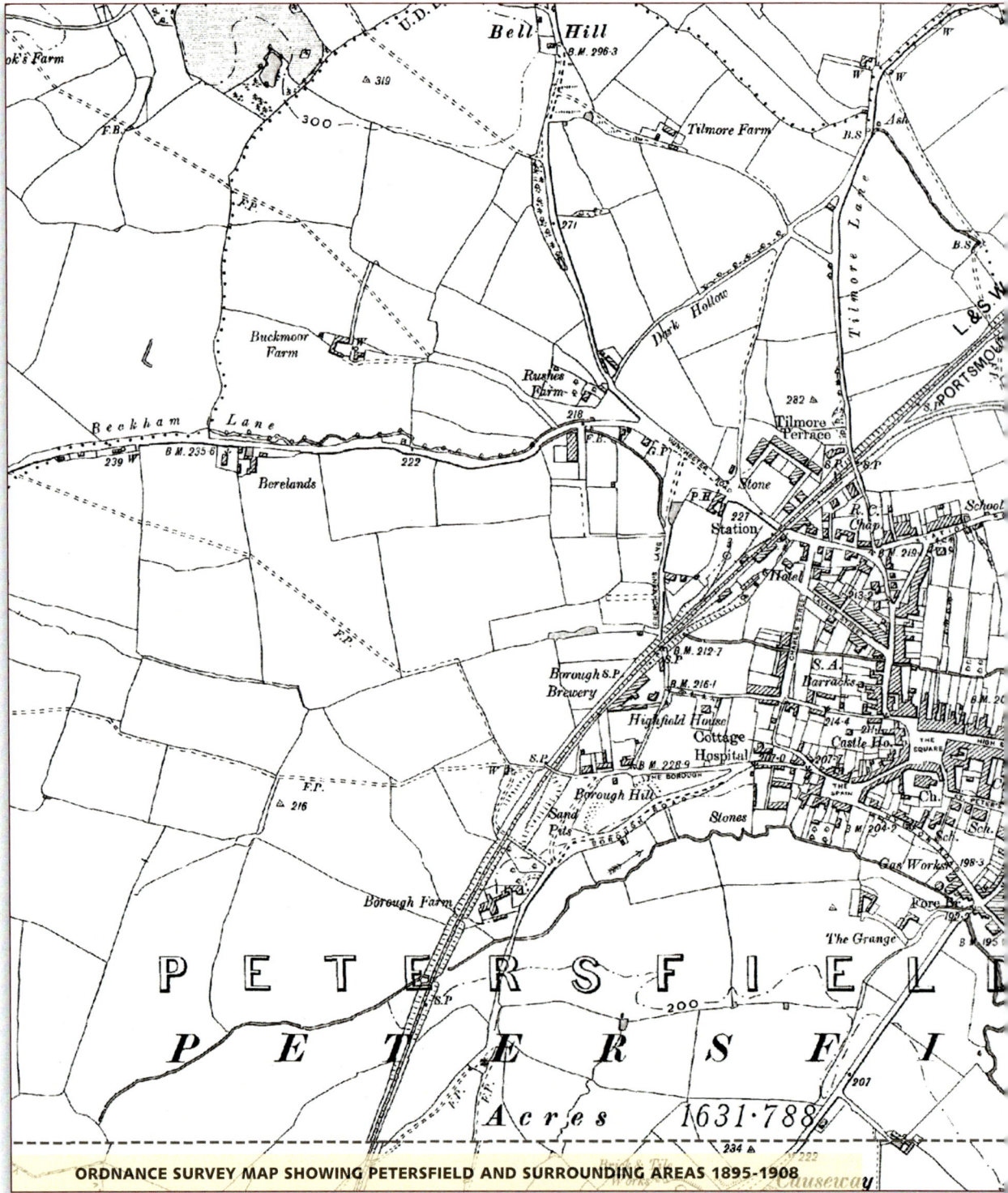

ORDNANCE SURVEY MAP SHOWING PETERSFIELD AND SURROUNDING AREAS 1895-1908

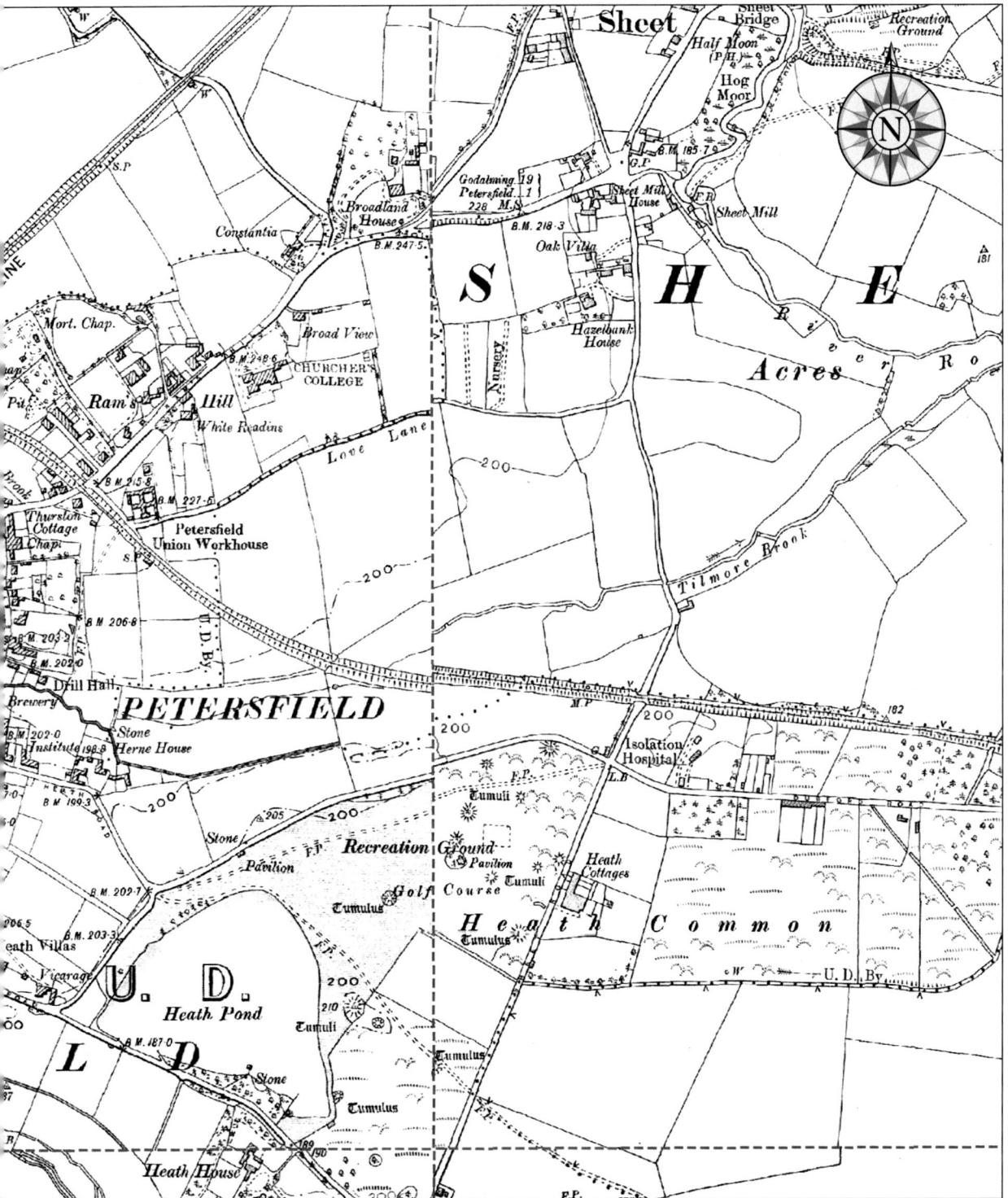

Sheet

Sheet Bridge

Recreation Ground

Half Moon (P.H.)

Hog Moor

B.M. 185·79

G.P.

F.B.

Sheet Mill

Sheet Mill House

Godalming 19
Petersfield 1
228 M.S.

B.M. 218·3

Oak Villa

Broadland House

Constantia

B.M. 247·5.

Nursery

Hazelbank House

S H E

Acres

River Ro

Mort. Chap.

Broad View

CHURCHER'S COLLEGE

B.M. 248·6

Ram's Hill

White Readins

Pit

Love Lane

200

Brook

B.M. 258

B.M. 227·6

Thurston Cottage

Chapl

Petersfield Union Workhouse

S.P.

200

Tilmore Brook

B.M. 206·8

B.M. 205·2

B.M. 202·0

U.D. Bdy

210

Drill Hall

Brewery

PETERSFIELD

MP

200

182

Isolation Hospital

L.B.

B.M. 202·0

Institute 198·8

Stone Herne House

200

F.P.

Tumuli

B.M. 199·3

200

Stone

·905

200

Recreation Ground

Pavilion

Golf Course

Heath Cottages

Tumuli

Pavilion

Heath Villas

B.M. 209·7

206·5

B.M. 203·3

Tumulus

H e a t h   C o m m o n

Tumulus

W

U.D. Bdy

Vicarage

U. D.

Heath Pond

210

Tumuli

L   D

B.M. 187·0

Stone

Tumulus

189
190

Heath House

200

F.P.

21

CHAPTER THREE
WALLS OF BRICK

GENTLY, over the centuries, Petersfield grew in importance and size. In the mid 16th century the town gave all the appearances of being run by a mayor and commonalty; in other words, the town governed itself. This was owing to its having developed with the assistance of only a light touch from the Staffords, the lords of the manor. To bolster the town's chances to gain independence in applying for a royal charter, a mace was purchased, which may well be the oldest in the country.

But change was in the offing, and on 23 July 1599, towards the end of the reign of Queen Elizabeth, Thomas Hanbury bought the letters patent for £216, entitling him to rents from the town, ponds, mill streams, running waters, rights of enclosure and of warren (rabbits) in the woods. Also, and this was perhaps more important, it gave Hanbury rights to hold Courts Leet, fairs, and markets, and to retain fines and dues. This led Hanbury to exert his rights over Petersfield, and to put its inhabitants in their place. He wanted suzerainty over those who 'unjustly pretend themselves to be burgesses of Petersfield'. This culminated in the case coming to court in 1608 and the court deciding in favour of Thomas Hanbury in 1610, which legally established his power over the mayor and the burgesses. It is interesting to note that the court concerned was the Court of the Exchequer - of which Hanbury was a judge.

THE TOWN MACE

The two-foot-long parcel gilt mace has presided over the affairs of the town since the reign of Queen Elizabeth I. It is clearly dated 23 March 1596 on the base (see below right) and is to be seen in place before the Town Mayor at all meetings of the Town Council.

THE TOWN MACE HEAD 2005
ZZZ04811 (Petersfield Town Council)

THE BASE OF THE MACE 2005
ZZZ04812 (Petersfield Town Council)

THE HANBURY LETTERS PATENT

The Letters Patent granted by Queen Elizabeth to Thomas Hanbury are still in existence. The document was purchased by Petersfield Area Historical Society in 1981 at Sothebys; it was lot 450 in the sale of 13 April 1981, and was secured for the town at the sum of £993.20. The document was presented to Petersfield Town Council, and is deposited in Hampshire Record Office, Winchester. The parchment was cleaned by the famous book-binder Roger Powell, and an oak scroll box was made by Oscar Dawson, who worked with Edward Barnsley. Edward Barnsley was an international figure in the world of high-quality furniture, and he donated the wood. A key fashioned in the manner of the head of the town mace was made by Terry Barnfield, an engineering instrument maker. A facsimile copy of the document is lodged in the Town Hall; it was photographed by Peter Dolphin.

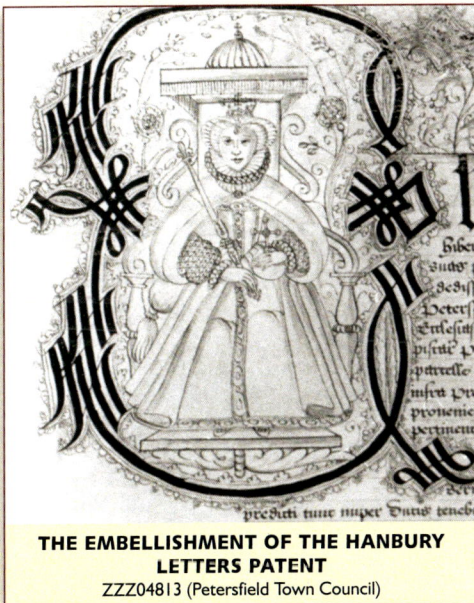

THE EMBELLISHMENT OF THE HANBURY LETTERS PATENT
ZZZ04813 (Petersfield Town Council)

OSCAR DAWSON WITH THE SCROLL BOX
ZZZ04814 (Petersfield Museum)

At about this time the town became a place to be reckoned with. What was subsequently known as Castle House was built on the west side of the Square; there have been many tales connected with it. There has always been a rumour, nothing more, that Queen Elizabeth I stayed in the house; if that was so, she must have been quite old, as the house is usually reckoned to have been built in 1593, only ten years before Elizabeth I died.

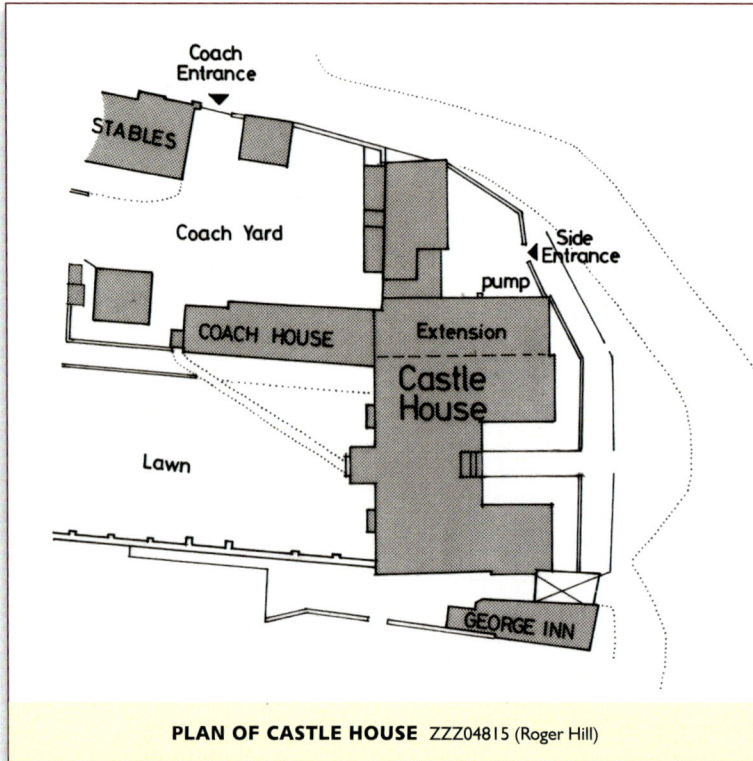

PLAN OF CASTLE HOUSE ZZZ04815 (Roger Hill)

would only be two days' work to fill the tunnels in when they were not of any further use. In all probability they would soon be past history, and would become the subject of tales of smuggling and assignations. At nearby Uppark there is a network of similar tunnels; they are well maintained and in good condition for all to see and experience.

When the Civil War came in the 17th century, it had been fermenting for at least 100 years. As a member told the House of Commons: 'It is strange how we have insensibly slipped into this beginning of a civil war by one unexpected accident after another as waves of the sea which have brought us this far and we scarce know how, but from paper combats, by declarations, protestations, votes, answers and replies we are now come to the question of naming generals and officers of an army'. When the Stuart Charles I succeeded his father James I, he proclaimed the Divine Right of Kings and locked horns with parliament over the question of raising money to run the country. The final straw was Ship Money to finance Charles's navy - this was bitterly opposed by parliament. The Civil War was the unavoidable consequence.

Another tale is that tunnels radiate out from Castle House, one to St Peter's Church, and another across the street to No 1 the Square. There is no reason for this to be some sort of fable, and there is indeed a logic in stories like this. Certainly the sun did not shine every day, and the streets were quite often muddy, and not surfaced as they are in these present times. It is well-established that this solution was widely applied throughout the country. Deep trenches would be dug along the route to be traversed; these would then be covered over to form a tunnel, so that the rain was kept out and shoes stayed dry. It is entirely possible that tunnels like this were constructed around Castle House, and it

NO 1 THE SQUARE

This is considered to be the oldest building in Petersfield. It was built in Tudor times, and is oak timber-framed with unusually close centres. As one would expect, the first floor jetties out over the ground floor of the building. It is thought to have been built as a farmhouse, possibly the Home Farm to Castle House. The most interesting feature is that instead of being in brick or the clunch that one would expect, the infill panels (noggins) are carried out in knapped flints. Over the years fires have necessitated the replacement of major timbers, which has considerably extended the life of this lovely building.

NO 1 THE SQUARE ZZZ04816 (Petersfield Town Council)

A MODEL OF A TIMBER-FRAMED HOUSE 2005 ZZZ04817 (Petersfield Town Council)

JOHN GOODYER

John Goodyer was England's first, and for a time foremost, botanist. He was born in 1592 in nearby Alton, and his life is commemorated with a plaque on Goodyers, a house in The Spain, Petersfield. It is appropriate that the town's expert historian, Mary Ray, now lives in the house. Goodyer was a friend of John Tradescant (the great naturalist and gardener), who gave his name to the species of plant called the tradescantia, one of which is known as Moses in the Bullrushes. He was also well-known to Elias Ashmole, who came to visit him in his 'Great Howse in ye Spain' (Ashmole went on to found the Ashmolean Museum in Oxford). John Goodyer's name is commemorated in the 40 species of goodyera, otherwise known as the jewel orchid. He was described as 'the foremost herbarist of his day'. His protection order during the Civil War, given by Lord Hopton, a general of the Royalist army, was discovered in 1907 hidden under the floorboards in his house. At the time of the Civil War crops were failing, and both Royalists and Parliamentarians needed his expertise. He died in 1664 and was buried in an unmarked grave within Buriton churchyard.

JOHN GOODYER'S HOUSE c1955 P48017

GOODYERS 2005 P48724k (Kenneth Hick)

The Civil War is generally reckoned to have begun on 22 August 1642, and by the end of that year Arundel, Chichester and Winchester had fallen to the Parliamentarians, led by Sir William Waller. Within the year Winchester was back in Royalist hands, but there were no battle lines as such; each side occupied certain towns, but not the land in between. Petersfield's fate was to be in the hands of whichever side happened to get there first, although distinct Parliamentarian sympathies were evident. On 24 November 1643 Royalist troops, on their way to take Arundel, left their quarters in the town, but were caught at Harting and three of them killed. Successful though the Royalists were in taking Arundel under General Lord Hopton, it was the Parliamentary roundheads who invested Arundel Castle on 20 December 1643, which led to a Royalist surrender on 6 January 1644.

By March 1644 Petersfield was Parliamentarian country, with Sir William Waller's army of some 10,000 troops being fed and watered in and around the town. They were on their way back from Arundel to Winchester and Basing House, both Royalist strongholds. They were also on their way to the Battle of Cheriton, some 10 miles to the west of Petersfield, perhaps the turning point of the war.

The Parliamentary army was at great pains to maintain a good name by not antagonising the honest citizens that they came across during their marches across the country. To keep the army in good order there were frequent courts martial. Two were held in Petersfield during December 1644 - whereabouts in the town we do not know, perhaps in the Town Hall, or in the function

A TYPICAL MARKET HALL c1650 ZZZ04819
(Titchfield History Society)

room of one of the major inns in the town (the White Hart or 22 High Street, then the Half Moon), or even in St Peter's Church.

Perhaps the uncommitted burgesses of the town had saved Petersfield from fire and the sword. Surely they must secretly have sided with the king, although they were outwardly Parliamentarian, and possibly this would have ensured that the Elizabethan mace was protected from the Parliamentarians, who would have melted it down to finance their campaign. What a tale that mace could tell about the Civil War in this corner of the County of Southampton, as was its title, and how lucky the town is to have what must be the oldest mace in the kingdom.

Many churches had their vicar removed during the Commonwealth and a man of more puritan sympathies installed in his place. If you consult the list of incumbents usually displayed in parish churches you may see the words 'Commonwealth Intruder' or simply 'Intruder' inserted after the appropriate entry. Such a list may be found in St Peter's Church. Buriton and Petersfield's rector from 1631

Fact File

At a court martial on 20 December 1644, one William Quincey was found guilty of theft and robbery and sentenced to be 'hanged by the neck until he be dead.' His corporal, Nicholas Read, who also took part in the robbery, was found guilty and sentenced to be paraded before his regiment, 'to be cashiered the army, his sword broke over his head, never to bear arms again in the Army.' It is believed that the two punishments were carried out on the same day at the same place, the Gallows Field, more or less where the Swan Street car park and the telephone exchange are today.

until 1645 was Benjamin Laney. (Later, on the restoration of the monarchy, he was appointed Bishop of Ely as a reward for his loyalty to Charles II whilst the king was in exile.) In 1645 Robert Harris (Intruder) was appointed pastor, and he conducted the affairs of St Peter's in a Presbyterian manner until 1660.

Although King Charles I was executed in 1649, the Civil War carried on until the Parliamentary victory at the battle of Worcester on 3 September 1651. Following this defeat, the future King Charles II escaped in disguise to exile in France. As he crossed the south of England he inspired numerous public houses to call themselves the Royal Oak, and en route to his embarkation point at Shoreham he probably made his first, but not his last, overnight visit to Petersfield.

1597 - 1631	PHILIP WALKER
1631 - 1660	BENJAMIN LANEY
1645 - 1660	ROBERT HARRIS (*Intruder*)
1660 - 1688	EDMUND BARKER
1688 - 1699	CHARLES LAYFIELD
1699 - 1732	WILLIAM LOWTH

THE LIST OF VICARS 2005 ZZZ04843 (Kenneth Hick)

JOHN WORLIDGE

A great-grandson of John Goodyer, John Worlidge was an important commentator on horticulture, but it is as an agricultural author that he was best known. He lived in what is now Worcester House, on the corner of Heath Road and Dragon Street - the house has a wonderful front door case (see right). Like so many, he had a vision for the future of agriculture, but his ideas and inventions were not always followed up immediately. Worlidge was nevertheless held in high regard for his views, and his books on topics such as a gardener's year, making cider, and bee-keeping, were well received. His best-known book, 'Systema Agriculturae', also had a number of reprints, as well as five updated editions, during the next 50 years. Jethro Tull is usually credited with the invention of the seed drill; but John Worlidge outlined the design of such a machine at an earlier date, but his design did not attract interest. However, we must remember that something the whole world takes for granted in the 21st century was the idea of a man from Petersfield. John Worlidge died in 1693, and there is a memorial to him in St Peter's Church.

THE FRONT DOOR OF WORCESTER HOUSE 2005 P48723k (Kenneth Hick)

Following the death of Oliver Cromwell, the Lord Protector in 1658 and the restoration of the monarchy in 1660, Benjamin Laney returned and reclaimed the title of Rector of Buriton and Petersfield for the Protestant cause, immediately handing over to Edmund Barker who was then appointed rector (1660-1668). He would doubtless have met King Charles II on the monarch's overnight visits to Petersfield on his way to and from Portsmouth to visit his Royal Navy and to inspect the defences of the dockyard. It is just possible that he also met the King's mistress, Louise de Kérouaille, who was considered worthy of the title The Baroness Petersfield.

LOUISE DE KEROUAILLE, BARONESS PETERSFIELD, GASCAR c1673 ZZZ04818
(Reproduced by courtesy of The Trustees of the Goodwood Collection)

Yes, Petersfield had a baroness. Born Louise-Renée de Penancoet de Kérouaille in September 1649 in Brest, western France, she was at the age of nineteen appointed maid of honour to the Duchess of Orleans. The duchess was Henrietta, sister of King Charles II of England. The king was said to be very tall and to have had very expressive large eyes. He was also a dedicated and skilful diplomat. In April 1670 Louise embarked at Dunkirk with the Duchess of Orleans, who was to meet Charles II in Dover before the signing of the Treaty of Dover on 1 June. He was infatuated, to say the least, with Louise de Kérouaille; he was to describe her as 'the only jewel I covet'.

'Madame Carwell', as the English pronounced her name, rapidly became the successful rival of Nell Gwyn for the King's affections; just as the King revelled in the coarseness of Nell, his appreciation of Louise's refinement, mental abilities and breeding knew no bounds. Louise bore King Charles a son, Charles Lennox, who took his first breath on 29 July 1672. Later he became the first Duke of Richmond, whose family seat is not far from Petersfield at Goodwood House.

In 1673 Louise was created Duchess of Portsmouth, Countess of Fareham, and Baroness Petersfield. With the great interest of King Charles in his navy at Portsmouth, one is left to wonder what significance those places held in the life of the king and his mistress. We have none other than Samuel Pepys to thank for the information that King Charles certainly spent nights at Petersfield!

After the death of King Charles II in February 1685 at the age of 55, Louise returned to live in France with her son by the late king, the thirteen-year-old first Duke of Richmond, who was subsequently deprived of his post of Master of the Horse. She died in Paris on 14 November 1734, having outlived Charles II by nearly 50 years, nearly three and a half times longer than she was his mistress.

THE ROYAL COAT OF ARMS ZZZ04820
(Petersfield Museum)

Fact File

The coat of arms which calmly hung above the Chairman of the Bench in the Petersfield magistrates' court was accepted for the authentic royal coat of arms until the court became home to the Petersfield Museum. The grant-aided restoration threw doubts on its authenticity; the royal motto 'Dieu et mon Droit', when cleaned, revealed an earlier motto, 'Per Mare Per Terras'; not only that, but the unicorn appeared to have been modified from the body of a dog (see ZZZ04820). Investigation is presently being carried out into its origins.

Vernacular architecture is governed by a number of constraints, such as local weather, what is available, and, of course, the ingenuity of the local builders. The area around Petersfield is no exception. Four details are worthy of particular mention. The first is galleting, a means of decorating and protecting the edge of the mortar bed between layers of bricks. Sometimes pieces of flint were used, and sometimes red iron pyrites chips, which incidentally gave the name garneting to the process. Galleting is found only in West Norfolk and along the North and South Downs. The second is a brick bond. Although there are many types of brickwork bond, one of the more unusual was what is commonly called the rat-trap bond. This was achieved by laying the bricks on edge rather than in their normal orientation. It made the bricks go further, but it made the wall less strong.

Our third building detail is mathematical tiles, an invention aimed at avoiding the brick tax which was imposed in 1784. They were a wall tile-hanging arrangement which looked convincingly like bricks, as the photographs show.

GALLETING 2005 ZZZ04821 (Kenneth Hick)

RAT TRAP BOND ZZZ04822 (Kenneth Hick)

MATHEMATICAL TILES 2005 ZZZ04823 (Kenneth Hick)

MATHEMATICAL TILES 2005 ZZZ04824 (Kenneth Hick)

Finally, we come to flints. Flints are often used in older houses, or indeed in modern character buildings. They can be used as they are, just as they come out of the ground, or they can be knapped with a scotching hammer. Knapped flints present the inside of the stone to the viewer. Jack Stubbington, a local brickwork expert, says: 'The blackest flints are the best, they are the least permeable and the hardest.' When building flint walls he builds up only nine inches at a time, otherwise the mortar slumps. 'I build in the mornings and point the flint in the afternoons,' says Jack.

The town was taking on a new shape as

A FLINT WALL 2005 ZZZ04825 (Kenneth Hick)

the medieval buildings were reaching the end of their useful lives. Durable bricks made possible the erection of some of the classic Georgian buildings that still grace the town.

A KNAPPED FLINT WALL 2005 ZZZ04826 (Kenneth Hick)

ALE BREWING

The name 'maltings' is one sure clue to the fact that the brewing of ale and beer has taken place in a town, and Petersfield is no exception. Amey and Luker were two very well-known brewing names within the town, but they were not alone. Many small public houses would brew their own beers for consumption by their customers. Malt is the pre-requisite for brewing; it is made from soaked barley, which is then left to sprout on large areas of floor. When sprouts first appear they are shovelled up and put into an oast house to be dried. There is an oast house among the outbuildings at Lords Farm in Sheet, and the old maltings still exists in Dragon Street and at Hattons Mead in Heath Road. The drying process produces the malt, which is crushed in a mill to produce grist. This is then mashed with water, and the starch that the mash contains is turned into sugar (the wort stage). Before around 1550, this was the stage when hops were introduced to turn ale into beer. After this distinctions were blurred and ale was used as a term for light beers. The wort is then poured into a fermentation vessel and yeast is added. After perhaps four days in this stage, any conditioning considered necessary is added. Then the beer or ale is put into one of the various sized casks: a pin holds 4½ gallons, a firkin 9 gallons, a kilderkin 18 gallons, and a barrel 36 gallons.

A BOX OF LUKER'S BEER BOTTLES 2005
ZZZ04827 (Petersfield Museum)

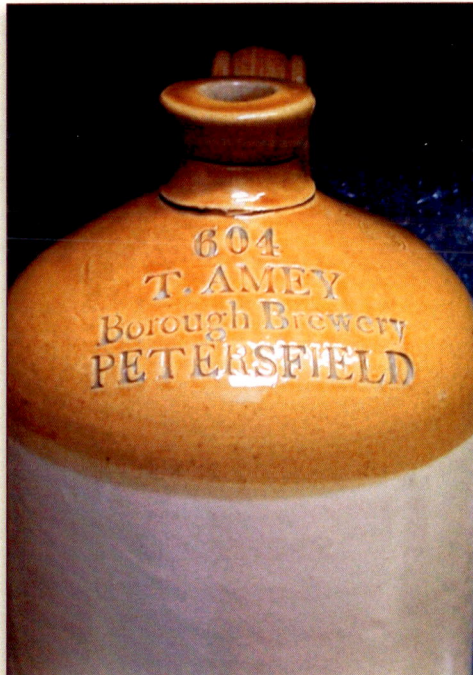

AN AMEY GREY HEN 2005
ZZZ04828 (Petersfield Museum)

During the 18th century the economy of the United Kingdom was gaining momentum, and industrialists were becoming rich. Some, indeed, were gathering their riches from abroad, on sugar plantations and suchlike, whereas others were making their money from industry in the midlands and the north. In Staffordshire a family called Jolliffe were a great success in industry and finance, so much so that they were looking for an opportunity to extend their influence into parliament. They accomplished this by buying the manor of Petersfield, and with it the right to send two members to parliament. In 1720 William Jolliffe had Petersfield House built just south of St Peter's Road, very close to the present police station; the site now houses the appropriately-named Jolliffe Court.

He obviously took a dislike to what he saw at the bottom of his garden, and had any vestiges of the tanyards and old mills moved out of his view by sealing off what is now Hylton Road and creating a gently sloping garden down to the stream. He completed his garden with water features, created by working on the stream, and making ornamental ponds which no doubt were stocked with fish. He then had a clear view down to his inherited Home Farm at the Grange, now home to the Grange Surgery. There was nothing unusual in this; throughout the country, lords of the manor were moving villages away from their view when building their own extravagant houses. The removal of the village around St Hubert's Church at Idsworth is a local example.

This school was built on part of the garden of Jolliffe's Petersfield House. The school was later redeveloped into dwellings which are now called Jolliffe Court.

THE SCHOOL 1898 41327

THE GRANGE 2005 P48725k (Kenneth Hick)

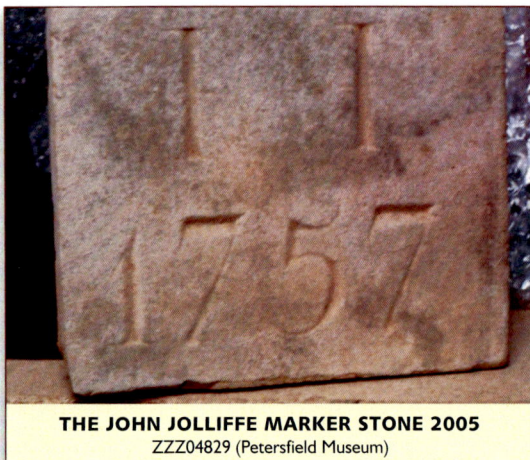

THE JOHN JOLLIFFE MARKER STONE 2005
ZZZ04829 (Petersfield Museum)

To aggrandize the entrance to the family home as it was approached from St Peter's Road (New Way), William Jolliffe provided £500 in his will, together with any further sums considered necessary, for the erection of a lead statue of William III. This was to be placed in the circus at the entrance to Petersfield House. He also had a stepped entrance to St Peter's Church constructed in the wall at the corner in New Way for his household's use. The steps are sometimes referred to as 'the Jolliffe Steps.'

THE JOLLIFFE STEPS 2005 P48726k (Kenneth Hick)

No trace of Petersfield House now remains, but the statue in tribute to William III is now a well-known feature: it holds court in the Square. Just one vestige remains to give a clue where the statue of William III originally stood in New Way. Inside the goods entry to the former Co-operative store in St Peter's Road, behind the white house, is a small section of substantial curved wall. A projection of that curve defines the position of the wall outlining the circus at whose centre stood the plinth and statue of William III.

THE SITE OF THE STATUE OF WILLIAM III, ST PETER'S ROAD 2005 ZZZ04830 (Kenneth Hick)

The small section curved of wall, projecting the circle, at the centre of which stood the statue of William III. New Way is now St Peter's Road.

THE STATUE OF WILLIAM III 2005 ZZZ04831 (Peter Greinke)

THE STATUE OF WILLIAM III

The statue of William III was placed at the entrance to Petersfield House in New Way (now St Peter's Road) in 1757. It was moved to its present position in the Market Square in 1812. This kind of monumental memorial is rare in England; Petersfield's well-known statue in the Square, described as 'Magnificent and Heroic deserving the admiration of the townspeople', was cast in lead during 1753 by John Cheere. It was originally erected in New Way as a result of a bequest of £500 by Sir William Jolliffe. Following its removal to the Square it remained in the ownership of the Jolliffes, later to become the Hylton family, but it was purchased by the then Urban District Council in 1911 for £125 (this sum also gained for the town the market rights and the Square). The statue was restored in 1913 with a new wrought-iron armature supported by a post from the horse's stomach to the top of the plinth. The cost was £225, which was raised by Inigo Triggs with public support. Further repairs were carried out in May 1929. Registered as an ancient monument on 3 March 1952, it was further restored in 1962-1963 following its acquisition by the Hampshire County Council. The wrought iron armature was replaced by one of bronze, and the under-support was taken away; the work was carried out in Chessington, Surrey. It was listed as a building of historical and architectural interest on 30 November 2001. Similar statues can be found in Bristol, Hull, Glasgow and Dublin. They are all in a very similar style to the statue of Marcus Aurelius in the Piazza del Campidoglio in Rome. They all portray the king minus stirrups and dressed as a Roman emperor; the Petersfield statue is even graced with a Roman nose.

With the lord of the manor laying claim to powers previously exercised by the mayor and burgesses of the town, there was cause for great resentment within the borough, which bubbled on over many years. Parliamentary election results were repeatedly challenged in the courts during the century that the Jolliffes held sway over the town.

At the same time, the name of Petersfield was becoming well-known as a staging post on the London to Portsmouth route. Towards the end of the 17th century, Daniel Defoe travelled from London to Portsmouth and passed through the town, which he described as 'a town eminent for little but its being full of good inns, and standing in the middle of a country still overgrown with a prodigious quantity of oak timber'. One hundred years later it was credited as being 'formerly a place of much greater consequence'.

During most of the 18th century the export of wool was forbidden, and with human nature being what it is, there was money to be made. In all probability Petersfield would have been one of the inland focuses of smuggling. Wool would have been gathered from the area of the Downs around the town and transported under cover of darkness down to the coast at Emsworth or Warblington. The ships would go through Chichester harbour mouth and head towards the French coast. On the right tide those very ships would bring in all the desirable goods that the nearby continent had to offer. Tobacco, brandy, wine, and for a time salt, were very sought-after in London, and they all attracted customs levies which were important to a balanced national budget.

JOHN SMALL II

In St Peter's burial ground there is one tombstone remaining upright. It commemorates the family of John Small, who was born in 1737 and died on the last day of 1826 aged 89 years. He was the second of four of that family and name. He came of a musical family who all played in the church orchestra; in fact, it is recorded that John Small II was playing the violin and reading music without spectacles during the last two years of his life. Good eyesight gives a clue to his fame as a cricketer. He would walk all the way to the Hambledon cricket ground on Broadhalfpenny Down for a match, and he formed a formidable batting partnership with William Beldham. He was one of the original members of Hambledon Cricket Club (Hambledon was the birthplace of cricket, and the rules of the game were made by the club). He took part in one of the most famous matches that was ever played against the England cricket team on 18 June 1777; it was for a wager of 1,000 guineas, and was won for Hambledon by an innings and 168 runs. Individual scores were not kept, but John Small was said to have played a significant part in the run scoring. On one occasion, playing for Hambledon, he carried his bat for three days in a match against the rest of England.

'The said John Small,
Wishes it to be known to all,
That he doth make both bat and ball
And will play any man in England
For five pounds a side.'

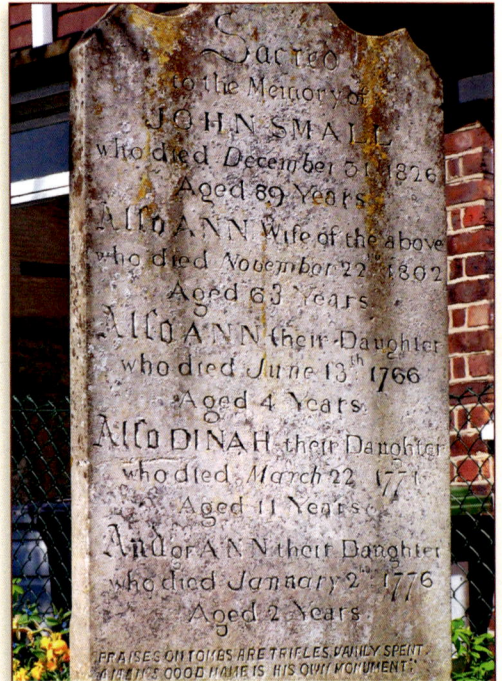

**THE TOMBSTONE OF JOHN SMALL II
PHOTOGRAPHED IN 2005** P48727k (Kenneth Hick)

The Fireplace in the Room of John Small, the famous Hambledon Cricketer, at 6 & 8 The Square

A Relic of Old Petersfield

Visitors to

NORMAN BURTON'S

Ladies' Wear Specialist

6 & 8 The Square Petersfield

are cordially invited to view this historic Room

AN ADVERTISEMENT FOR NORMAN BURTON'S
ZZZ04832 (Petersfield Town Council)

HAMBLEDON, BROADHALFPENNY DOWN CRICKET MEMORIAL 2005 H405701k (Kenneth Hick)

THIS STONE MARKS THE SITE OF THE GROUND OF THE HAMBLEDON CRICKET CLUB CIRC. 1750-1787

It is not hard to imagine packhorses leaving various barns in the area around the town and making their way to join others at Buriton, going on through the woods to Rowlands Castle, down through Westbourne to the coast, then off-loading. Perhaps the return journey would take place on the following night, and the children on the route were told not to look out of the windows (as in the Rudyard Kipling poem, 'And watch the wall, my darling, while the Gentlemen go by!'). Those horses found tired out in the morning had not really been ridden all night by the fairies, as folk tales would have people believe; it was far more likely that they had been carrying contraband. The transport of smuggled goods along the road to London could be very profitable for all concerned, and that included the squire and the priest,

Fact File

Around 1720 the Heath Pond came into being. For many years the people of Petersfield had dug peat from the Heath to the extent that some of the diggings collected water and formed ponds, thanks to springs below the surface. The resulting boggy area brought cattle to drink, and in some cases they became stuck fast and drowned. Determined to end this state of affairs, many citizens came to help to create one big pond. This they did by excavating the whole 22 acres of marshy land, tipping the spoil to create what is now called Music Hill. Little did they know that they were creating a beauty spot, sought out by many from far and wide - the more so since the advent of the car.

COWS IN THE HEATH POND ZZZ04833 (Petersfield Museum)

not to mention the farmer, the carter and even the shepherd. There was always a way of earning a dishonest penny for people in the country, even if it was only for turning a blind eye.

The prevention officers had only limited success, but when they did they had a good way to advertise that success, which at the same time gives us some idea of the route taken by the smugglers. The choice of locations for the gibbets for those caught, convicted and hanged in chains are recorded; they were on the Downs of West Sussex, with further gallows at Rowlands Castle and at Rake on the London Road, some four miles north of Petersfield.

In 1710 the London to Portsmouth road was in a bad state: 'By reason of the Multitude of Carriages to the said Town of Portsmouth for the Use of the War and also other Carriages travelling through the said Highways are become ruinous and for the space of Nine Months at least in every Year almost impassable'. This situation pleased neither the parishes nor the road users. With the London to Portsmouth road carrying much more traffic owing to the burgeoning of the Portsmouth dockyard, the situation was critical. The Portsbridge to Sheet Turnpike Act was passed through parliament in 1711. This meant that a company or trust could be set up to run stretches of road of a much higher standard than was possible under the old state of affairs, and they could charge for the use of their roads. The trust could build tollhouses and bars in order to collect dues with which to maintain the roads. The aim was to reduce the gradients over the South Downs and to bypass the narrow village of Sheet.

THE POND c1960 P48032

HIGH STREET 1880 ZZZ04834 (Petersfield Museum)

This is the earliest known photograph of Petersfield.

Previously, under the provisions of the Highways Act 1535, every householder had to give four days labour per year, and every ploughland held by a farmer attracted a levy of four days a year for a cart and two men. Needless to say, this provision was not successful. This impractical arrangement came to an end, and the parishes then became responsible for the upkeep of roads within their boundaries. This arrangement worked quite well for minor roads or tracks, but major roads would be cut up by the narrow

THE RED LION c1955 P48044

iron-tyred wheels of an increasing number of carts and carriages as they moved heavy loads for long distances. A cartoon of the early 1700s showed a sailor with a wooden leg walking along a road and being asked by a stagecoach driver: 'Do you want a lift?' 'No', replies the sailor, 'I want to get there quickly.'

As a result of the Portsbridge to Sheet Bridge Turnpike Act, the slope at the top of Butser Hill was reduced somewhat with a cutting, and the route up the hill from the north was straightened. This was regarded as suitable employment for the French prisoners of the Seven Years' War (1756-63). Their quarters probably gave their name to Frenchman's Road to the west of the town.

As for Sheet, a new stretch of road was constructed leading from the toll bar by the river to the top of Town Lane, and a milestone was erected telling the weary traveller that there was only one mile to go to the inns of Petersfield. Making Ramshill passable in all

A TURNPIKE MILESTONE 2005
P48729k (Kenneth Hick)

weathers was another aim of the Turnpike Trust; this hill, just outside the town, had always created problems for travellers.

TARMACADAM

Well-constructed roads were usually formed on the John MacAdam principle of keeping the soil beneath the road construction dry. Essentially his method consisted of a cambered base and a wearing surface of small stones. These were made impervious with a colloidal mixture of clay, gravel and sand; it was all the better if the construction was carried out in dry weather. Dusty in dry weather, roads made in this way were nevertheless looked upon as a godsend compared to the poor quality roads that preceded this manner of construction. For the first time it became possible to maintain high speeds, with horses galloping the distance between stops. The 20th-century use of bitumen as a binder and a most effective waterproofer gave to the world the word tarmacadam, and with it much improved roads.

COLLEGE STREET 1906 54399

The roads were kept in a good state of repair, enabling high speeds to be maintained by the best of coaches. Indeed, the coaching record from Liphook to Petersfield, albeit set in the 1800s, was 23 minutes, and the Regulator coach held the London to Portsmouth unbeaten record of nine hours. The arrival of the railway in 1859 signalled the end of stagecoaches, which until then still had to provide a connection between the rail terminus at Godalming and Portsmouth. It also brought Sheet turnpike to its financial knees - it was wound up in 1871. By 1877 the responsibility for all highway maintenance passed to a local highways board.

The Sheet tollhouse became the village's post office before its demolition in the 1930s, but in 2005 its hemispherical two-part door can still be seen in good condition, not a mile away from its original position, gracing the front of an old cottage.

But why have a turnpike from Sheet Bridge to the bridge to Portsmouth in the first place? The answer was quite simple: a coach or cart would have difficulty finding a way round the toll bars without a costly and roundabout route.

Over the years the town challenged the results of a good number of parliamentary elections on the grounds of the qualifications for franchise. In essence many of the townspeople wanted to run the town for the town, and not at the behest of the lord of the manor, but the election of members to parliament was the tip of the iceberg.

SHEET, THE TOLLHOUSE DOOR 2005 S107701k (Kenneth Hick)

This curved door was built by a cooper, or barrel maker.

RICHARD DENSHAM

In 1799 Richard Densham was ordained minister to the Petersfield Congregational Church. He was a prolific preacher, possessed of considerable energy. The record states that in 1800, early in the morning of 2 August, he preached at Harting to a congregation of 90 people. By eleven o'clock he was in Petersfield, and then he travelled to East Meon to preach at two o'clock. Not content, he then rode nine miles to Rogate to preach to an assembled early evening crowd of nearly 500 people, where he received a very rough reception and rotten eggs abounded. His fervour for preaching the word of the Lord led to his being included in a book entitled 'Evangelical Biography'. This was regarded as no mean accolade at that time. He was a man of unquestioned and unfailing Christian faith, and instigated the opening of chapels at Harting and Petersfield in September 1801. He died the morning after being thrown from his gig on the way to preach at Haslemere; he lies beneath a memorial at the eastern end of the present United Reformed Church. Such was the antipathy between the town's denominations that the bells of St Peter's Church were rung loudly in an attempt to drown out the prayers at his funeral.

COLLEGE STREET 1898 41323

The Congregational Church can be seen centre right. It is now the United Reformed Church.

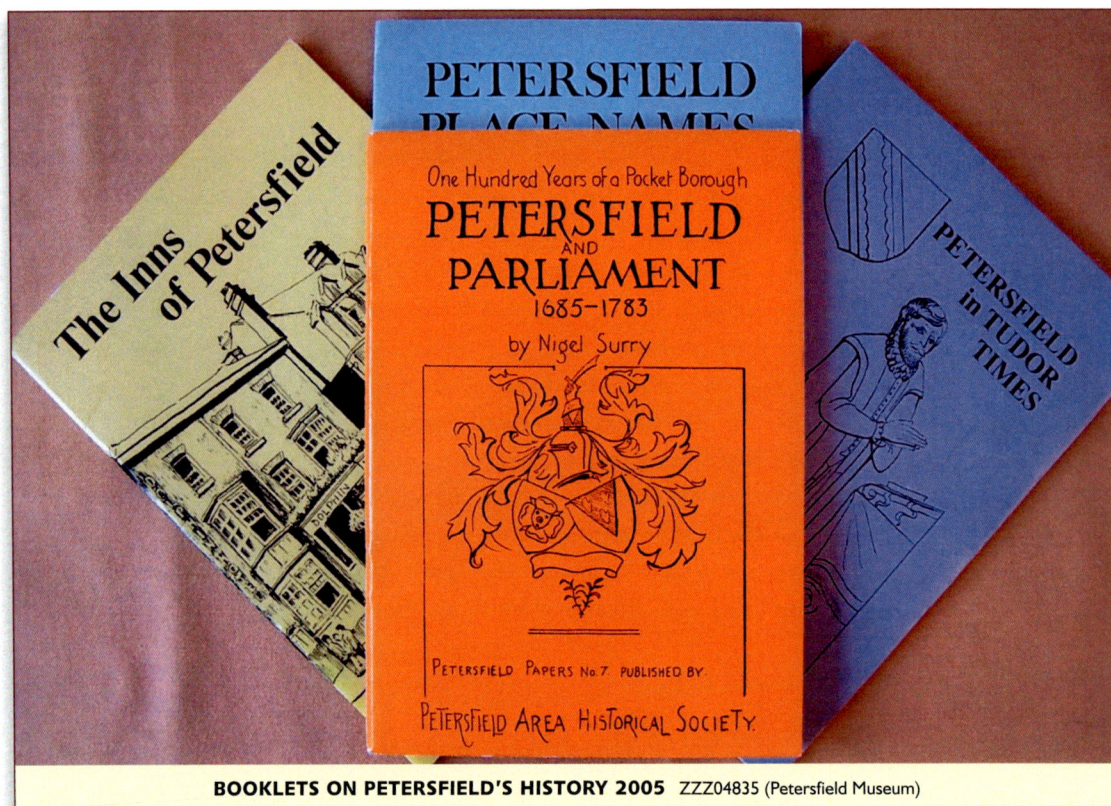

BOOKLETS ON PETERSFIELD'S HISTORY 2005 ZZZ04835 (Petersfield Museum)

An excellent publication published by the Petersfield Area Historical Society, 'Petersfield and Parliament 1685-1783' by Nigel Surry, catalogues the representation of Petersfield. By the time in question, the mayor was inevitably the lord of the manor's man. In the 1774 election it was alleged by the defeated candidate that James Stowell 'pretending to be the Mayor of the Borough acted partially and unfairly as returning officer.' The successful candidate, William Jolliffe, in enumerating his expenses, included 'Beer given away at Election £6 and Sundries at Public Houses £20'.

Exasperated, the citizens of Petersfield tried for one last time to unseat the members of parliament after the election of 1819. The Petersfield Case was to be a turning point in British democracy. Heard before a committee of parliament in 1820, the town challenged the result of the recent election, whereby two members, Hylton Jolliffe and Lord Hotham, were returned to parliament at the behest of the lord of the manor. It was he who had decided which people should have a vote, based on some rather unsound criteria. The people of the town took the matter of these criteria to parliament, but on 16 June 1820 the case was found for the sitting members, Hylton Jolliffe and Lord Hotham. Petersfield was declared by some to be 'the rottenest borough in the country.' Nevertheless, the people of the town did not let it rest there, and appealed the result. The appeal was successful, and the jubilation in the streets of the town on the evening of 30 May 1821, when news of the success reached Petersfield, was recorded in the daily national papers of the time.

The town had stood up to the lord of the manor; wherever British democracy is discussed or debated, the part played by the good people of Petersfield should never be forgotten. The Petersfield Case is famous in the annals of British democracy, and it led directly to the abolition of Pocket or Rotten Boroughs by the Reform Act of 1832. It is interesting that when the present Town Council adopted the style of Town Mayor in 1973, it was as a tribute to the action of the burgesses of the town in their fight for British democracy over 150 years before.

By 1820 coaching days were at their pinnacle; the railways were on the horizon and people were looking for the means of travelling to other parts of the country. Coach routes were established over long distances (London to Manchester is one example), so long that the journey was undertaken in stages - hence the word 'stagecoach'. Petersfield was a name well known to travellers on the Portsmouth to London Road, for it provided accommodation for overnight stops and refreshment, together with a change of horses. The names of the coaches were redolent with speed, and were often inspired by the then latest technology. The coach's arrival would be announced from the top of College Street or at Golden Ball Street (Sussex Road) by the post horn of the stagecoach guard; that must have caused the pulses to quicken.

Three days during the week there was a coach on the Portsmouth to Oxford route called the 'Oxonian'. The route taken by this stagecoach is not

A MAP OF PETERSFIELD 1831 ZZZ04884 (Petersfield Town Council)

This was one of a series made to bolster the Reform Act of 1832. The borough boundary is in blue.

known, but very likely it was routed through Winchester and Newbury. Other names heard on the road to London, such as the 'Royal Mail', 'Hero', 'Victory', 'Nelson', 'Rocket', 'Regulator', 'Royal Blue' and a strange one, 'Accommodation', would all be on the lips of hotel and innkeepers in the Town.

THE SQUARE c1750 ZZZ04836 (Petersfield Bookshop)

Fact File

Horn lanterns were equipped with moulded cow horn, as at that time there was no glass that could be shaped to fit the radius of the candle lantern. Cow horn was boiled, the centre removed, and the translucent outer sheath slit open. Whilst it was still hot it was laid out, pressed into flat panels, cooled and cut to size. These panels were fitted into the channels around the outside of the lantern; they let the light through and at the same time stopped any wind from blowing out the candle.

A HORN LANTERN 2005 ZZZ04837 (Petersfield Museum)

In fact, the 'Accommodation' was not so much a stagecoach, but a van with five horses that left the Globe Inn at Oyster Street in Portsmouth and arrived at Aldersgate Street in London sixteen hours later. Research has yet to establish its purpose, but indications are that it was a kind of next-day parcel delivery service. The yellow 'Nelson' coach was a night coach, and averaged eight miles an hour. It changed horses twice before Godalming - these changes took place at Petersfield and at Liphook. Normal London to Portsmouth journey times, after the creation of the turnpikes, were nine hours by day and twelve hours at night. The Royal Mail coach took ten hours, but could ignore the turnpike charges.

The Red Lion, the Dolphin, the White Hart and the Green Dragon were famous coaching inns on the Portsmouth to London route. Their workers would also be aware of which coach would be in next and which horses to have ready for the change. In 1857, two years before the railway reached Petersfield, the 'Rocket' four-horse coach left either the Red Lion or the Dolphin Inn 'every morning at 10 o'clock to GODALMING, in time for the 1pm train, returning on the arrival of the 1pm train from Waterloo', according to a contemporary notice.

THE OSTLER

An ostler, or hostler, would be the stableman at the inn or the hotel. He would be busy from early morning to late at night. A man who knew horses well, he would receive the horses with the stagecoach, unharness them, take them to the stable yard, and set them to the water trough. The waiting new horses would be harnessed up ready for the coach to be on its way with new or refreshed passengers. The watering horses would need to be inspected to see if the skill of the farrier was needed, and they would be fed. The horses would then be turned out to graze in the hotel's meadows close by. The names Outer Drum Mead, Angel Mead, and Castle Mead all commemorated the names of inns or hotels in Petersfield. The ostler's lot was to endure all weathers. He would have to wait until the last coach had arrived and the horses settled for the night before it was his turn to 'hit the hay', though on occasion there would be a coach arriving during the night. Summers meant long days at work, as the summer timetable went on all the hours that light granted. Some stages would be completed during the hours of darkness, the moon and footpads allowing.

CHAPTER FOUR

TOPPING OUT

"INTERNATIONAL STORES"

BBS
INGSMITH

COLLEGE STREET 1898 41324

THE END of the Napoleonic Wars with France resulted in hardship for many in and around Petersfield. The army and the Royal Navy threw many of the combatants back into the lives that they had previously left. Many from the Royal Navy were recruited into the ranks of the excise men, where they contributed successfully to drastically reducing this particular form of tax evasion. The troops who left the army appear to have swelled the number of footpads along the road to London and in the surrounding countryside; even so, the number of people living on the parish increased alarmingly. These people were not just poor, they were destitute, and were quite often pushed from one parish to another.

Their lives were sheer misery. Take the case of Mary Cousens, pregnant in Havant in 1822. The justices conveyed her to 'her lawful place of settlement, to wit Hayling North', where the baby was born. After she married one George Parfit, the justices saw fit to move the couple and the baby to Parfit's lawful place of settlement, Liss. At a later date the overseers of Liss established the facts appertaining to the infant and sent the child back to Hayling North, 'her lawful place of settlement'. The child thus became a pauper and an orphan by the same order, signed by the Petersfield justices.

The number of paupers was nigh on overwhelming. A far more effective system was needed where efficient means could be found to provide for the poor. Poorhouses then sometimes performed the same function as Job Centres do today - but for children. Many a young boy found himself being transported to the industrial midlands and the north to be apprenticed to work in one of the new wool or cotton manufactories. Conditions in many poorhouses were described as being 'at best appalling'.

Petersfield Workhouse, still in Love Lane, is now converted to provide affordable housing (Rookes Meadow, right). It was built in 1835 following the previous year's enabling legislation, which encouraged parishes to join together in a union to construct worthwhile accommodation for the destitute. Previously, each parish had borne responsibility for the poor in its own particular way. The union which built the Petersfield Poor Law Institute consisted of the parishes of Bramshott, Buriton, East Meon, Empshott, Colemore, Froxfield, Greatham, Hawkley,

Langrish, Liss, Petersfield, Priorsdean, Privett, Sheet and Steep. These would have been the ecclesiastical parishes. The total population of these parishes in 1911 was 12,561.

ROOKES MEADOW 2005 P48731k (Kenneth Hick)

THE SPAIN 1898 41326

65

The workhouse master would have been expected to command respect and to be sober, active and diligent. On his shoulders would be placed the responsibility of appointing an appropriate workhouse matron with similar attributes, and any other staff required. In 1835 Petersfield's workhouse provided places for 78 inmates and ten officers. The Union Overseers' Boxes are to this day preserved in Petersfield Museum in St Peter's Road.

Every morning some of the inmates would wend their way into the town to work in the houses or the inns. Their path lay across the meadow which is now crossed by Tor Way, then alongside the Tilmore Brook, turning sharp right where there is still a footbridge, and finally down Folly Lane to the High Street and the inns and houses of the town. Others capable of harder work would go to work on the farms to earn their living.

In 1900 the guardians agreed to the overseers building a chapel on land immediately to the northeast of the workhouse. This little-known lovely chapel is still in use to this day - the Petersfield Evangelical Church own it now.

With good coaching links to London and other towns, Petersfield was a centre of road communications. With the construction of railways countrywide, it was a town waiting for an overdue miracle, and that is just what happened.

Fact File

The workhouse was hit by a German bomb on 21 November 1940 at about 11.30 in the morning. Eight people were killed, including Mr and Mrs Ixer, the workhouse master and matron. The bomb fell on the front of the workhouse, destroying the entrance hall and the master's apartment. Seven people were killed instantly: four inmates, the porter Mr Weeks, the workhouse master, and Emily Rutter, only 23 years old. Mrs Ixer, the workhouse matron, died later that day from wounds that she had received. It was the work of just one bomb, perhaps one left over from a stick dropped elsewhere. It is said that the bomber, thought to be a Heinkel 111, made a circuit of the town and dropped its barrel of death indiscriminately.

THE PATH FROM THE WORKHOUSE TO THE TOWN 2005
P48732k (Kenneth Hick)

On 4 January 1859 the railway arrived; it was to join Godalming and Havant stations, and as a consequence, it was possible to travel from London Waterloo to Portsmouth direct. Previously a journey from London to Portsmouth entailed one of two options: to go to Croydon and then to Brighton, with a change there onto the South Coast line to Chichester and Portsmouth, or to follow the line of the Admiralty telegraph through Basingstoke, Eastleigh and on to Gosport, from where it would be necessary to take a pinnace to the King's Stairs and into Portsmouth.

The London Brighton & South Coast Railway had made an agreement for the London South-West Railway to use the rails between Havant and Portsmouth, but obviously the LB&SCR were not to be trusted. The first train to arrive at

THE STATION c1930 ZZZ04838 (Petersfield Museum)

the Havant junction was manned by a useful number of gangers, all adept at handling themselves. The inevitable fight ensued, with lumps of coal being the major weapons. After a lot of bad language and a few cuts and bruises, the train withdrew to Godalming; meanwhile, a number of telegraph messages were exchanged and a clear understanding developed.

LAVANT STREET c1965 P48064

To get from the Market Square to the station involved walking the length of Chapel Street and then along Station Road. So in the 1880s Lavant Street was built, creating a link between the Drum Inn and the station forecourt, and giving an impressive entrance for visitors to the town. Most of the houses which were built at that time in Lavant Street are still there, although most have had shop extensions added to their fronts.

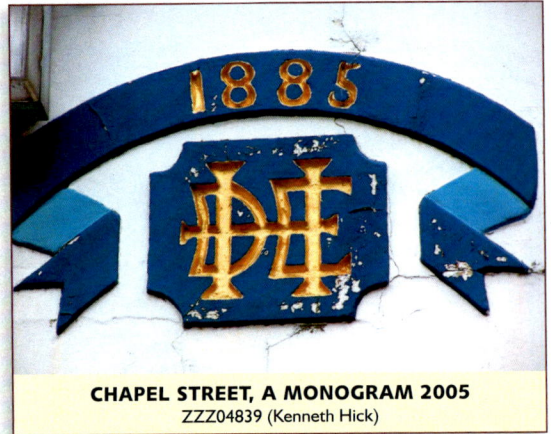

CHAPEL STREET, A MONOGRAM 2005
ZZZ04839 (Kenneth Hick)

DAVID EDWIN HOBBS

David Hobbs was a well-known name in Petersfield. He was a farrier (his signboard reads 'Shoeing and Jobbing Smith') who carried out his calling in the building which is now a bakery, behind the cake shop in Chapel Street opposite the Sue Ryder charity shop. Along the pedestrian way into the central car park, the wall on the right still has a ring to which horses were tethered whilst waiting to be shod. A good number of house deeds in the town will include his name, as he was a trustee of the Ancient Order of Foresters (Petersfield). This benevolent society pursued a policy of buying any land in the town in which nobody showed any apparent interest. To this day the area in front of Lloyds Bank, popular with charity stalls, belongs to the Ancient Order of Foresters. David Hobbs also owned the Swan Implement Works, which stood in the north-east corner of Castle Yard car park. He joined the Urban District Council, and was elected Chairman in 1921-1923. It should be understood that he was no relation to the well-known brothers Ernest and Gilbert Hobbs.

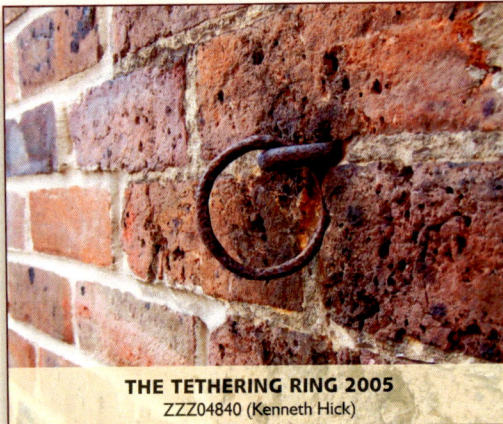

THE TETHERING RING 2005
ZZZ04840 (Kenneth Hick)

Now it was full steam ahead for the town. Within 24 years Chapel Street was developed, the Station Hotel was built, Station Road, Sandringham Road, and Osborne Road were built up, and the proud houses that stand to this day along Station Road appeared, although not all of them featured stables at the back for ponies and traps.

If we look up at many of the shop premises in Chapel Street and Lavant Street, we will see many dates of the 1880s, and monograms too - one of these is on the Age of Elegance shop (ZZZ04839, page 68). DEH stood for David Edwin Hobbs, who lived in The Spain and carried on a farrier's business next door; he also owned this building, later known as the International Stores (ZZZ04841, below).

It was not just new roads that were developed, but also houses were built to satisfy the demand for substantial property. Areas apparently remote from the railway station were regarded as desirable. Heath

D E HOBBS'S PREMISES IN THE EARLY 1920s ZZZ04841 (Petersfield Museum)

Road was constructed, and over part of its length some of the largest homes were erected, with the Heath and its pond in the foreground and wonderful views towards the South Downs.

THE STATION HOTEL 1985 ZZZ04842
(Petersfield Museum)

Fact File

The Station Hotel was built on the site now occupied by retirement flats. It provided the ideal commercial hotel for salesmen or commercial travellers wanting to cover the area around the town. Here they could stay for the week, and hire horses or a carriage from the attached stables and go out each day to visit the villages and sell their wares. At the end of their week they could take the train home and be ready to cover another area in the week that followed. The commercial travellers would take around tins of Brasso and Zebrite, or samples of materials of all colours, or almost anything that a shopkeeper could want on his shelves, in order to drum up sales.

A careful study of the maps of the time can only impress upon the researcher the impact that the coming of the railway must have had on the geography of the town. Even without the number of houses that the railway spawned, Petersfield would never be the same again, for with the railway came the grand building that is Petersfield Station.

Plans were put in hand to construct a railway to Midhurst and on to Pulborough, which had a connection with London Victoria. But there was yet another plan to link Petersfield with Winchester, which would have meant Petersfield becoming an important railway junction, and demands for even larger goods yards. The Midhurst line opened on 1 September 1864, and for 90 years plodded its way via stations at Nyewood, Elsted, and on to Midhurst for Pulborough and Chichester, until its closure on 5 February 1955. That evening the last train, driven by Mr F Goldsmith of Horsham, was seen off by the Chairman and Clerk of Petersfield Urban District Council, respectively Mrs A A Hayes and Mr H H Creedon.

As it was, the goods yard denied the town its cricket pitch, which had to be moved to the Heath in 1858; here a thatched cricket pavilion was built as some compensation. There were other details that needed to be considered; building the bridge in Tilmore Road would necessitate the steepening of the road between Station Road, and the bridge would inconvenience the horses and carts delivering to that part of the town.

The railway bridge in Frenchman's Road was built at a low-lying spot which was, and still is, subject to occasional flooding. This meant that the bridge was built with only restricted headroom, and over the years this obstruction has been the cause of many embarrassed lorry drivers' headaches. Some mishaps have led to the temporary closing of the railway in order to assess damage to the bridge. Streams were more difficult to divert; they always take the line of least resistance, which means following the valleys, and they will have followed their previous routes.

An interesting result of the coming of the railway was the Long Road. The name is interesting in that it was the name given to the road by Sheet schoolchildren as they walked to school from Tilmore and the cottages by the reservoir.

Fact File

The Long Road runs straight alongside the railway line between School Lane and Kingsfernsden level crossings. The road was constructed in order to avoid a third level crossing for a lane that ran south easterly from Lords Farm to halfway along Kingsfernsden Lane. To a little child, the featureless Long Road seemed to go on for ever into the distance.

FROM TILMORE 1906 54393

SHEEP STREET 1906 54400

The railway was routed away from the town centre to avoid expensive land acquisitions. It is significant that it can be seen to have defined the western boundary of the town in 1859. All the buildings on the west side of the railway can be said to have been erected since that date, except the farms at Buckmore, the Borough, Berelands, Rushes and Lords.

A whole new horizon beckoned, with officials able to travel every day from home to destinations such as London, Guildford, and Portsmouth Dockyard - and what a lovely place Petersfield was to come home to at night. And the change came so rapidly: yesterday a long tiring journey by stagecoach, the next day only two hours to London by train.

Banks had operated in the town for a good number of years, and carried out their business in various buildings. One of the most interesting buildings to house a bank is No 15 High Street, on the south side. This house is typical of the symmetrical style of the 1700s, with the front door placed right in the centre

NO 15 HIGH STREET, THE DOOR TO THE VAULT
2005 ZZZ04845 (Kenneth Hick)

of the frontage, and a very sturdy building it looks. In the early 1830s it became home to Mr Butterfield's Bank, which finally closed its doors in 1851 when the bank ceased trading. There were not sufficient funds available to take out the strong room, and it remains there to this day.

In 1865 the London and County Bank built its new bank on the site of No 4 High Street. Its Italianate style and its bulk caused a stir; not only did its style shock the worthy inhabitants of Petersfield, but also the brightness of its yellow brickwork. This bank has served the people of the town for over 100 years, and now that the coloured brick has toned down, it lends an air of authority to the town centre. A further bank came to Petersfield when Barclay's Bank opened a branch at No 10 the Square on 18 February 1929.

Fact File

Inside No 15 High Street there lurks a bank vault from the past. Too expensive to remove when the building changed hands, it has been an item of curiosity ever since, and now houses washing machines and ironing boards in its role as a 21st-century utility room. It is a house that can be proud of its past - it now offers Bed and Breakfast to the town's visitors.

PETERSFIELD

Fact File

Maps do not give just a bird's eye view of the ground - they also have important height and level information. Surveyors needed reference points to work from, and these reference points are called bench marks. Not always obvious, there are many about the town. The photograph shows a simple one on the stallriser of No 6 High Street, at 208ft 6in above mean sea level.

THE UPPER LINE IS A BENCH MARK 2005
ZZZ04846 (Kenneth Hick)

HIGH STREET c1965 P48078

These were indeed stirring times. Within the course of ten years, Petersfield had a railway station, a police station (built in 1858) and a corn exchange (see ZZZ04847, page 77). It also included street lighting in its list of amenities. The gas-works had opened in 1862 with a view to providing lighting in Petersfield homes and street lighting both in the town and in Sheet village.

The Petersfield and Selsey gas-works were in Hylton Road; but all that is left on the site of the gas-works, now Tesco's car park, is a regulator valve in a compound next to the pathway into Hylton Road. Bert (Shirty) Passingham, who worked at the gas-works, was always proud of his claim that on Christmas morning he was at the gas-works very early in order to make sure that the gas holder was riding high. The higher the gas holder, the better the pressure for cooking the Christmas turkey, bringing cheer to all. Bert used to live at Chalton windmill and cycled into work every day.

The Petersfield gas-works was associated with two others, the ones at Emsworth and Titchfield. In time the works became a branch of the Portsmouth Gas Company, and gas was piped from Hilsea gas-works at Portsmouth, bringing an end to the gas production retorts at Hylton Road. Today the town is connected to the national gas grid which brings natural gas from the North Sea to our homes and factories.

The militia had always played an important part in the life of a Hampshire town, and over the years volunteer platoons and battalions were a source of pride to the inhabitants. Since time immemorial the Heath had been a training ground for military manoeuvres, and the track across the top end of the Heath was named Exercise Way. But there was always the need for out-of-the-weather accommodation for small arms tuition and foot drill.

THE POLICE STATION 2005 P48733k (Kenneth Hick)

THE CORN EXCHANGE

This was built to provide a covered building where corn (wheat, barley, and other cereals) could be bought and sold; its building must indicate an ever-burgeoning corn trade, and the conversion of fields from cattle to cultivation. The carts and wains can be imagined blocking the entrances to the town and creating havoc in the Market Square as they unloaded their sacks of corn. These would be judged, sold to the highest bidder, reloaded again, and taken away by the purchaser. This was very hard work; a sack of barley would weigh one and a half hundredweight. Latterly the Corn Exchange

THE CORN EXCHANGE c1927 ZZZ04847
(Petersfield Museum)

was used as a public hall, and even as a substitute church whilst St Peter's was being improved in 1874. In 1922 it housed the first performances of the Petersfield Operatic Society, and in 1928 the Corn Exchange was converted for retail use.

For a short time a building within Clarendon Yard (see map on page 27), by the footpath to Moggs Mead, served this purpose, but the consolidation of the British Empire, combined with the pressing needs of the late Victorian Boer War, dictated that something bigger and better was needed. This requirement was a nationwide need, and drill halls were built throughout the land. A national programme was placed in the hands of Prince Arthur, the Duke of Connaught, and so many drill halls were titled the Connaught Drill Hall. In Petersfield the availability of the old maltings in Dragon Street provided a heaven-sent opportunity for a hall large enough in which to hold parades. It was also big enough for small arms and machine gun stripping down and maintenance training.

THE MALTINGS 2005 P48734k (Kenneth Hick)

MARKET SQUARE c1955 P48008

Fact File

For many years The Maltings was known as the Drill Hall, and living quarters were added for the sergeant major in charge and his family. Together with the Corn Exchange, it formed the backbone of the town's cultural life. When the Petersfield Musical Festival was founded in 1901, the Drill Hall was the only venue in the town large enough to hold the number of singers that made up the massed choirs involved. In the First World War it was one of the numerous town buildings used as a barracks for troops waiting to go to France. During the Second World War, garages were built to take large guns in excess of 25 pounds, together with their towing limbers. In 1969 it was bought for £62,000 by Post Office Telecommunications as a centre for the external engineering vehicles and their appropriate stores. When no longer needed by British Telecommunications, it was sold for residential development and resumed its historical title of The Maltings.

Together with the bold Victorian developments went new urban demands for better standards of hygiene. Large conurbations inevitably led to outbreaks of disease. Mr Morse's clever development of the telegraph code, named after him, enabled newspapers to spread the word of disease and death quickly throughout the land. Changes were on their way.

MARKET SQUARE 1898 41314

The cholera outbreak of 1863 in Chelsea had drawn the whole country's attention to the need for better drainage and water supplies. Outbreaks of typhoid and other water-borne diseases were becoming more frequent, with the concentration of urban cesspools seeping into many private wells. These city concerns were now reaching the smaller country towns such as Petersfield. Mr Bazelgette's pattern of London water treatment and sewage disposal was providing an excellent example for all to follow. Two 96.5m-deep artesian bores were drilled at Sheet to provide a source of potable (drinkable) water, and a reservoir was built at the highest spot nearest to the water pumps. This was at the top of Reservoir Lane. This water has a temporary hardness of 18.2 degrees.

The Local Joint Sanitary Board was then in a position to lay foul sewers to take water to the lowest point in the town. This was into the River Rother at the far end of Sandy Lane, now known as Durford Road, where a sewage works was constructed. Those Victorian sewers and the sewage works are still in use today, naturally with updated improvements. The fact that they have withstood the test of time speaks volumes for their Victorian designers and constructors.

Once again the town found itself in the familiar situation of one day having a creaky old pump, with luck inside the house, and the next day having water which was potable, connected, and came out of a tap, or possibly two taps. These considerable improvements were carried out during the period from 1884 to 1886; they did away with many of the town's cesspools and other unsanitary methods which had been in use up to that time.

The Redistribution Act of 1885 led to the extinction of the Borough of Petersfield in that year. A Town Trust was formed, in whose hands were left the civic regalia. There are currently investigations going on to ascertain the number of relics handed over to the trust at that time. One piece of regalia that they received was the town mace. It took many years to have the mace restored to the town, 44 years in fact, before the Urban District Council received it back from the Hylton family in 1929.

After a hiatus of 10 years in the government of the town, the Petersfield Urban District Council was constituted with nine members in 1895. It had the Town Hall in the Square in

THE SQUARE 1910 ZZZ04848 (Courtesy of Derek Leach)

This rare photograph shows the sign of the Golden Horse Inn and, bottom right, a sewer manhole giving access to the town's new sewers.

which to meet, which also provided cover to the market stalls underneath. What precipitated the demolition of the Town Hall, together with Pince's School and the offices of the Hampshire Post, we may never know. Nevertheless, that demolition in 1898 opened up the view of St Peter's Church from the Square.

THE TOWN MACE 2005 ZZZ04849 (Petersfield Town Council)

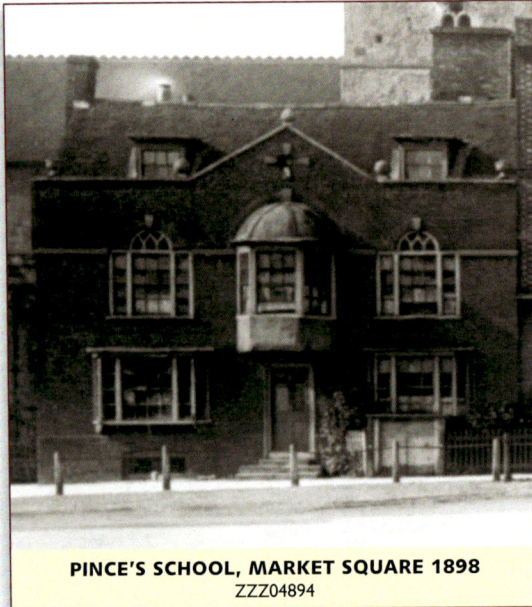

PINCE'S SCHOOL, MARKET SQUARE 1898
ZZZ04894

Fact File

When Pince's School was demolished in 1898, Petersfield lost one of the most elegant houses that it had ever known. Built in the reign of Queen Anne, its symmetrical frontage had great charm; it was the last building of the group to remain standing when the demolition of the Town Hall and the newspaper office took place. Now, in the 21st century, the appearance and the detailing of the front of this building would be cherished, and firm measures taken to ensure its conservation. Pince's School ended its days as an auctioneer's showroom.

The manner in which animals were slaughtered, and housed whilst at market, brought forward demands from the government for cleaner market surfaces and the limewashing of all carts coming into and out of the market.

Much of the limewashing was carried out in The Spain, and carts coming in from the south-easterly direction would be taken through the shallow cart-wash in the Heath Pond, where the boardwalk is now situated.

THE SPAIN, SHOWING HYLTON HOUSE IN THE CENTRE c1965 P48071

NEIGHBOUR THE GROCER'S c1900 ZZZ04850 (Petersfield Museum)

This shop was to become Forrest Stores, and is now the Edinburgh Woollen Mill.

The Market Square was concreted after much discussion between various government departments and the then Urban District Council. This enabled the market site to be well washed after the cattle market every Wednesday - this was all part of the country-wide drive to improve the health of the nation.

The bells of St Peter's rang in the 20th century, a century which was to witness the biggest changes that the town can ever have had forced upon it. Many changes came about with the Jolliffe family's decision to cut its ties with Petersfield and sell up its property in the town. It owned many houses around the town centre, but most importantly it owned the Square, the rights to hold a market there, and 'the Horse'.

At the sale of the Hylton estate in 1911, the Urban District Council bought the market rights, the Market Square and the statue of King William III for the princely sum of £125. By then the statue was in a poor state of repair, with King Billy leaning forward in a perilous position. A well-known local architect, Inigo Triggs, worked to raise the

MARKET SQUARE c1950 P48007

money that was necessary to restore the statue, and it was removed to the workshops of Messrs Singer & Son of Frome. The restoration, which included the replacement of the wrought iron armature inside the horse and a support between the horse's stomach and the plinth, was carried out for £225. The restored statue was finely unveiled with much ceremony on 3 September 1913.

Firefighting had been dealt with in an organised way for many years, but on the basis of amateur efforts, sponsored by insurance companies. The insurance cover would be validated by a fire mark attached to the front of the building concerned, and its presence meant that a fire in that building would be dealt with by the company's fire brigade. The town's second recorded chief fire officer was (Captain) Mr W P Jacobs, who joined the Petersfield Fire Brigade on its formation in 1890 when he came to the town from the Isle of Wight. He founded the estate agents W P Jacobs in Lavant Street in the year that the Urban District Council was founded, 1895.

CASTLE HOUSE AND THE MARKET SQUARE 1898 (BEFORE THE CONSTRUCTION OF THE HURDLE HOUSE) 41315

WILLIAM PERCY JACOBS

THE MARKET c1900 ZZZ04851 (Petersfield Museum)

- A PUBLIC-SPIRITED MAN

W P Jacobs was born on the Isle of Wight on 7 February 1865. The founder of the firm of auctioneers and estate agents which became Jacobs & Hunt, William Jacobs came to Petersfield in 1887 as an assistant to a local estate agent, Mr Alfred Williams. After the death of Mr Williams, William Jacobs opened his own estate agency, W P Jacobs (his sign is in clear view in this photograph). He joined the Urban District Council in 1909 and served continuously for 37 years, which included being chairman five times, a record not likely to be surpassed. He joined the fire brigade when it was formed in 1890, and was later its captain for eighteen years.

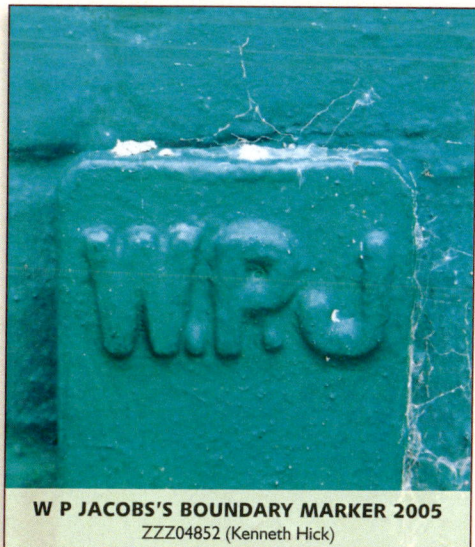

W P JACOBS'S BOUNDARY MARKER 2005
ZZZ04852 (Kenneth Hick)

THE HORSE-DRAWN FIRE ENGINE c1900 ZZZ04853 (Petersfield Museum)

The fire engine was horse-drawn with a steam engine (steamer) on board to pump water through the hoses and on to the flames. A request for the fire brigade would entail calling all the firemen from their homes or places of work by the bell, which was fitted to the chimney-stack of a building opposite Woolworth's in the High Street, and it would be the job of one of the men to gallop the horses from their field to the fire station. That fire station still exists today, serving as the public toilets in St Peter's Road.

Word has it that on one occasion the horses were out working in the fields, and so a lorry was hitched up to tow the steamer out to East Meon. Rounding Red House corner, the lorry went too fast for the steamer, which shot the fire coals out of the firebox;

THE FIRE CALL-OUT BELL, HIGH STREET ZZZ04854 (Petersfield Museum)

the steamer had to be stopped and the fire-coals returned to their proper place. There is no written record of this occurrence.

Fire engines were not confined to the town of Petersfield, but were also needed much further afield. In November 1904 the fire engine was called to Westbury House, close to West Meon, at 3 o'clock in the morning. As can be imagined, by the time a telegram had been sent to Petersfield, the alarm bell sounded, the horses collected, steam raised, and then galloping nine miles from Petersfield, it was a question of just damping down the ruins.

Yet another fire, this time at East Meon, is well recorded; the fire destroyed six thatched cottages on Monday 20 June 1910.

Monday was always washday, and coppers were lighted to heat the water; at about 8.30am, the chimney of Mrs Smith's copper caught fire, and the fire spread to adjacent cottages. Within one and a half hours the fire engine was on the scene, and water was pumped on to the remaining ruins from the nearby infant River Meon. 'Captain Tew controlled the fire ground.'

In 1925 the steam fire engine was replaced by a motorised vehicle. It was too large for the fire station, and the station was turned into public ladies' toilets. At the same time the hurdle house in front of St Peter's Church was converted for use as gentlemen's toilets.

PETERSFIELD'S FIRST MOTOR FIRE ENGINE c1925 ZZZ04855 (Petersfield Museum)

THE FIRE AT LUKER'S BREWERY 1934 ZZZ04856 (Petersfield Museum)

There have been a number of building fires over the years, one of which was the fire that destroyed the empty Luker's Brewery in College Street on August Bank Holiday Sunday, 1934. The ruined Antrobus Almshouses (1620s), which were attached to the brewery, were given the final coup de grace in the fire. The site was redeveloped as a wartime forces home from home, and is now at the centre of the Tor Way junction with College Street.

On 6 January 1947 an after-dark fire at Nos 6-8 the Square burnt down Norman Burton's general drapery shop. This caused much shock throughout the town; so much so, that the following

NOS 6-8 MARKET SQUARE 1898 ZZZ04895

Here we see Norman Burton's as it used to be, before the fire.

THE MORNING AFTER THE NORMAN BURTON'S FIRE 1947 ZZZ04857 (Petersfield Museum)

morning saw the staff in front of the ruins in tears. The old building was recognised as one of historic importance - and it included the room of John Small, the famous Hambledon cricketer. A new building was built on the site in the late 1950s, which is now a cake and coffee shop and a hairdressing salon.

Further major fires have taken place over the years, one of the most spectacular being the fire at Petersfield Timber Company in Hylton Road, where firemen had to take precautions against exploding tins of paint and volatile adhesive. There has also been a fire at No 1 the Square, the oldest building in the town, and more recently at Lyndum House, an historic High Street house. Another

notable fire resulted in the destruction of the thatched Cricket Club pavilion on the night of 17 November 1973.

Education has very deep roots in Petersfield; it is home to three independent schools and a state comprehensive school, fed from surrounding junior schools. The town has also played host to one of the early National Schools on a site in Sussex Road.

One well-known school, Churcher's College, was endowed in the will (dated 1722) of Richard Churcher in the sum of £3,000 when he died in 1723. After a period of discussion and negotiation, a site was purchased opposite the Black Horse, at the northern end of what is now College

Fact File

Firemen were issued with ornate helmets in order to protect them from harm. They were manufactured in large quantities, and every fireman was issued with one. Brass helmets had to be polished, and so some fire authorities would have had a chromium-plated version which always looked smart and did not need polishing.

A FIREMAN'S HELMET ZZZ04858 (Colin Langrish)

Street. The imposing Georgian college was built in 1729, in what is known locally as Stoneham Village, with the aim of tutoring boys of Petersfield in mathematics and navigation. Richard Churcher probably made his money in the East India

PETERSFIELD SCHOOL BOARD PLAQUE 2005 ZZZ04859 (Kenneth Hick)

The plaque is dated 1894.

Company, and realised the need for boys to be apprenticed to masters of ships whilst making their voyages to and from the East Indies. Unfortunately, the boys thought otherwise; it proved necessary to institute a variation to the will and the original idea was abandoned.

Eventually the building in College Street could not cope with the needs of the school, and new premises were opened on what was at that time the edge of the town, at the top of Ramshill. A new Victorian Gothic style building (1881) was commissioned, and today it still stands, much extended and meeting the needs of 621 pupils. For some years the old cottage building was used as a hotel, before becoming council offices.

The college had a strong tradition of tuition for the special services' examinations,

OLD CHURCHER'S COLLEGE 2005
ZZZ04860 (Kenneth Hick)

This stone bears the date 1729.

and in 1905 was one of the first public schools to have an Officer Training Corps. Another of the school's traditions is in the special study of music and the arts; these have always been taught to a high standard here, and the pupils are encouraged to perform

CHURCHER'S COLLEGE c1955 P48022

The OLD COLLEGE HOTEL
College Street, Petersfield

A fine old Georgian Residence with a Picturesque Garden, beautiful lawn and tennis court

Situated at the junction of Station Road and College Street, within 8 minutes' walk of the Railway Station and easy access to the
GOLF LINKS & HEATH

Electric Light

Garage

From London ... 55 miles
From Portsmouth 17 miles
From Winchester 19 miles
From Haslemere 12 miles

Telephone 34.   MOTORISTS ESPECIALLY CATERED FOR.   Proprietress—E. ADAMS

ADVERTISEMENT FOR THE OLD COLLEGE HOTEL 1935 ZZZ04861 (Petersfield Town Council)

in public. It is interesting to note, in a book on history, that one of the country's most notable archaeologists, Sir Stuart Piggott, was educated at Churcher's College and took his early steps in the science on Petersfield's Heath. Another ex-pupil was Tommy Rose, who in the 1930s became one of the country's most distinguished flyers. During the 1980s the college became co-educational, and at the same time ceased to be a boarding school.

Another famous school is Bedales, situated just outside Petersfield at Steep. It was founded at Haywards Heath in 1893 by J H Badley. In 1898 the first girls were admitted, making it one of the oldest co-educational boarding schools in the country. In 1900 the school moved to Steep, and since then the children of many famous parents have come to realise the value of a top-quality liberal education. It houses the renowned Olivier Theatre, a building of high architectural quality. Over the years a good number of ex-pupils of Bedales have become internationally famous, particularly in the arts, including the renowned bookbinder Roger Powell; the furniture designer and maker supreme, Edward Barnsley; and the film star Daniel Day-Lewis.

ST PETER'S CHURCH, THE INTERIOR 2005 P48735k (St Peter's Parochial Church Council)

MAP OF PETERSFIELD 1922 ZZZ04883 (Reproduced by courtesy of Hester Wagstaff, Petersfield Bookshop)

The cenotaph at the eastern end of the High Street and the Post Office had only just been erected.

EARLY in the 20th century two sisters from Petersfield attended the Mary Wakefield Westmorland Festival in Kendal, possibly the first competitive music festival in the country. So impressed were they by the festival's ethos that they came back to Petersfield determined to replicate the experience there. The sisters were Edith and Rosalind Craig-Sellar, and, building on the pattern laid down by Mary Wakefield in Kendal, they sought the support of keen musicians and a man of influence, John Bonham-Carter. The result was the Petersfield Musical Festival of 1901, at which six choirs came to compete against each other by singing a test piece from 'St Paul' by Mendelssohn. As we have already seen, the only venue large enough was the former Drill Hall in Dragon Street, now called The Maltings.

Except for the years during the First World War, this venue saw the festival through to 1936; then the new Town Hall (which had opened in October 1935) became the new venue for the orchestra and singers in a purpose-built hall at the rear of the building. Now called the Festival Hall, it was erected specifically with funds raised through the efforts of many people, but most of all by Dr Harry Roberts. Within the Festival Hall his efforts are commemorated by a drawing of him by the nationally recognised local artist Flora Twort, which is illuminated during performances there.

A DRAWING BY FLORA TWORT OF DR HARRY ROBERTS 1947 ZZZ04862 (Petersfield Town Council)

There is a story of the Drill Hall days related to the author by Sir Adrian Boult. The music being performed required bells in the score. Unfortunately, the tubular bells had not been ordered, and so Dr Boult (as he was then) walked across the road to the gas works in Hylton Road and set to work with a hacksaw to cut two pieces of pipe to the correct length for the notes required. He felt very pleased with the result, only to read in the following week's paper the efforts of a reporter with a sense of humour, who announced to all that 'the gas pipe was played by Dr Boult'.

Many aspiring nationally known conductors have used the festival as a stepping-stone in their musical careers. Others were established figures in the world of music, such as Sir George Dyson, Dr (later Sir) Adrian Boult, Dr Sydney Watson and Gordon Mackie. Gordon conducted the festival for just five years (1965-1970), and inspired the singers by his introduction of two choral works by Verdi, his 'Requiem' and 'Four Sacred Pieces', as well as the 'Te Deum' by Berlioz. At that time he was considered destined to be a world-class conductor - he had been entered for the Dimitri Mitropoulos competition in New York; but he was killed in a tragic road accident at Waterloo Station.

The Petersfield Musical Festival thrives to this day. It is interesting to note how life goes around in circles: the Mary Wakefield Westmorland Festival also thrives into the 21st century, with Mr Robin Orr as its chairman - Robin Orr knows the Petersfield Musical Festival very well, as he conducted the local Fernhurst Choral Society in the festival in the early 1960s.

In 1910 the Urban District Council considered that some of the town's street names, although quaint, were inappropriate, and changed Cow Legs Lane to Station Road, Nine Post Lane to Windsor Road, Sandy Lane to Durford Road, New Way to St Peter's Road, Back Lane to Swan Street, Golden Ball Street to Sussex Road, and Horne Farm Lane with Exercise Road to Heath Road. One incongruous street name of recent years is Meon Close. The River Meon is not within the Petersfield watershed - in fact it rises to the south of East Meon, and then turns sharply to the west to reach the sea in Southampton Water.

No history of any town could be written without a reference to the Great War of 1914-18, the war to end all wars. Petersfield became an overspill for Aldershot and Bordon (which is nearer to the town). Soldiers were billeted everywhere; Grace Hutson, writing

COLLEGE STREET 1906 ZZZ04893

This workshop of H Macklin used to stand where the entrance to Barham Road is now.

A MILK LORRY ZZZ04863 (Petersfield Museum)

South Eastern Farmers' lorries were famous for their London milk runs.

HIGH STREET 1898 41319

for the Hampshire Magazine, said that even the saleroom at Jacobs & Hunt became a barracks, with early morning parades being held in Charles Street. She recalled army soldiers leaning at the doorway smoking, and making the acquaintance of any young ladies who might be passing by.

More poignant was the recollection of George Inkpen, who was a telegram boy during the First World War. It was his job to go by bicycle and take orders telegraphed from the War Office down to the horse collection centre at Bolinge Hill. He then used to see the requested number of horses being taken to the goods yard and put on trains to go to the fields of Flanders. He recalled that some days he had to cycle down to the collection centre three times.

The deaths in the First World War of 100 of the town's young men are recorded on the cenotaph in the High Street, the equivalent of one of the dreaded telegrams delivered to a home in the town every fourteen days. The name of H Norris was added to the bottom of the north-facing panel in 1927. Things would never be the same again.

THE CENOTAPH 2004 ZZZ04864 (Peter Greinke)

The cenotaph in the High Street commemorates those who died in battle but whose remains lie elsewhere. It is of unusual and classic appearance; it was designed by the architect Harry Inigo Triggs, who had travelled and studied in Italy. The detailing is borrowed from the eight blank panels in the Medici chapel in Florence; on these panels are carved the names of the town's dead of the First World War. (Plaques were added after the Second World War commemorating the 54 young men who died on duty away from home during that conflict). After much deliberation over an appropriate location for the town's memorial, it was erected by the mason Andrew Perryman of Dragon Street in its present position early in 1922 - a position in the Square was discounted.

In the wake of the war, under the auspices of the Housing Act of 1919, the country set about building 'homes fit for heroes'. The first of these were built in Noreuil Road, which was named after a little village of some 100 inhabitants near Arras in France. Petersfield had adopted the village to help with its reconstruction, and a letter thanking the town for gifts of parcels of clothing and coloured wall maps to brighten the schoolroom was signed by J Nicholai, the schoolmistress at Noreuil.

The Electricity Supply Act of 1919 gave rise to an application by Dr R J Cross, Mr T A Crawter and Mr C W Seaward, who wanted to form a company to supply electric light to Petersfield. The plan was for a generator on land located to the rear of the Volunteer Arms (now Meon Close), with a frontage on Frenchmans Road. (Note that the company was only to supply electric light, not power). With houses having only 40-watt lamps, it is unlikely that a supply greater than 20 kilowatts would be required. Tom Crawter's house, Clare Cross, was the first house in Petersfield to be lighted by electricity.

HIGH STREET, CLARE CROSS 1898 41319v

Clare Cross was the first house in Petersfield to be lit by electricity.

Nevertheless, there was enough power to supply the Electric Theatre with the town's first film shows. The first cinema stood at the corner between Chapel Street and Swan Street - in fact, the demolition of the Swan public house made way for the Electric Theatre. That first cinema was replaced by the Savoy Cinema in 1935, and is now a nightclub.

SUSSEX ROAD, F E LEACH'S GREENGROCER'S SHOP
ZZZ04865 (Courtesy of Derek Leach)

Fact File

One of Petersfield's first electric street lights is still in position at the side of Caffe Nero.

ONE OF THE FIRST ELECTRIC STREET LAMPS
2005   ZZZ04866 (Kenneth Hick)

SAM HARDY

For many years, from the early 1900s up to the Second World War, Sam Hardy was looked upon as the squire of the town. He ran a pack of hounds, and cut quite a figure in hunting pink; the more so when the hounds were brought into the Square before heading off down Sheep Street into the country. The hounds were kept in kennels next door to the Jolly Sailor public house in the Causeway. The main building where the food was stocked and meat boiled for the hounds' food is still there, and the photograph shows an appropriate ridge-end ornament from the roof. There were two dogs, one at each end; one was stolen, the other is now in safe-keeping. When not dressed in hunting pink, Sam Hardy could cut quite a dash as an entertainer. Complete in highland regalia, he was well known for his renditions of the songs of Harry Lauder, who was a personal friend.

HOUNDS IN SHEEP STREET 1928
ZZZ04867 (Petersfield Museum)

**A RIDGE-END ORNAMENT OF A DOG
FROM THE KENNELS 2005**
ZZZ04868 (Kenneth Hick)

Industry was making itself felt in the town. One of the first was the Petersfield Laundry, built in 1905 in Frenchman's Road, where it still functions today. Another laundry was built at the end of Sandringham Road, but it ceased to function in 1919 after the First World War.

Flextella was set up by its parent company, Portsmouth Steel, in two sheds situated at the south end of their present premises in Frenchman's Road. To this day they are hard at work in vast premises on the same site, manufacturing 21st-century commercial fencing. The company's proudest boast is the manufacture and installation of camel-proof fencing for the Middle East. Today sports centres are key customers of the company. Now known as J B Corrie Fencing, the firm is hoping to re-locate within the town.

ITS RUBBER LTD ZZZ04869
(Petersfield Museum)

In 1919 the ITS Rubber Company (Ingwar, Tufford & Smith) was founded, and took over the premises then recently vacated by the laundry in Sandringham Road. They manufactured the concave-convex rubber shoe heel under licence from the ITS Rubber Company Inc of Ohio, USA. Mr Arnold Levy

MINIBRIX c1930 ZZZ04870 (Petersfield Museum)

was company chairman, having seen the future for the product in the United States. He hailed from Krottingen on the border of Lithuania with Prussia; he was determined to prosper, and was prepared to travel the world searching for that prosperity.

Itshide, a product of the ITS Rubber Company, was developed as a rubber-based boot and shoe soling material; it sold in a world-wide market. It was joined in 1927 by Minibrix, best-selling rubber building bricks, enjoyed by children all over the world. The 1950 Korean War brought a need for improved boots for members of the British army, and Itshide were called upon to supply the answer. Their laboratory responded to this by developing the Commando sole, which to this day is still regarded as the best product of its kind. Incidentally, the need for copious supplies of water to cool the machines in the factory led Itshide to sink their own water supply borehole, discovering a water-bearing aquifer at 212 metres; this was used to supply a reservoir and a tall water tower on the factory site.

Arnold Levy died in September 1955 and the company became a subsidiary of the Michael Colston Group, producing rubber components for Colston dishwashers and for the automotive industry. The factory is no longer there, and has been replaced by housing. There is no commemoration of the company in the town save the Town Mayor's badge of office, which was donated by the company in 1969 to celebrate 50 years of manufacturing in Petersfield.

CLEMENT ATLEE AND HAROLD WILSON VIEW MINIBRIX 1949 ZZZ04871 (Petersfield Museum)

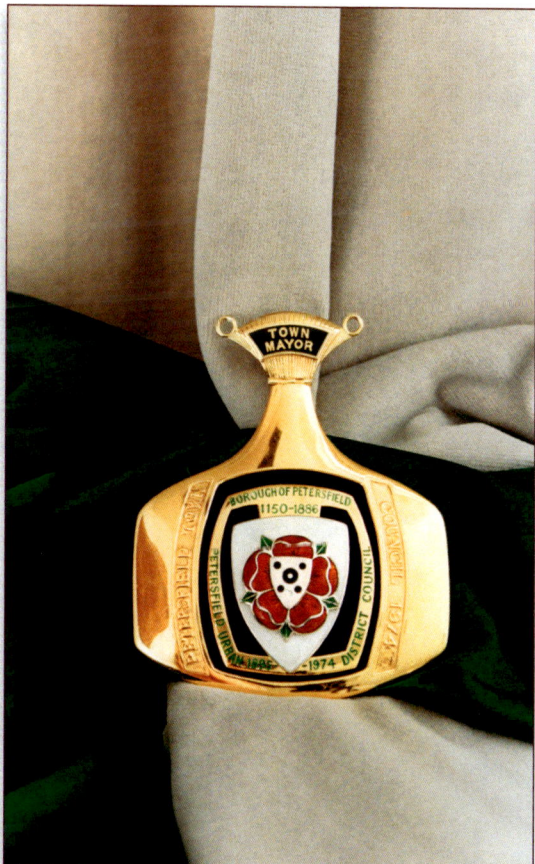

THE TOWN MAYOR'S BADGE OF OFFICE ZZZ04872 (Petersfield Town Council)

Fact File

The Town Mayor's handsome badge of office, worn with its chain when on official business in the town, is fashioned from 9 carat gold. At its centre, on a white shield, is the town badge in enamel, around which is recorded the civic history of Petersfield: 'Borough of Petersfield 1150-1885, Petersfield Urban District Council 1895-1974, Petersfield Town Council 1974'.

THE MAGNETO TELEPHONE
ZZZ04874 (Petersfield Museum)

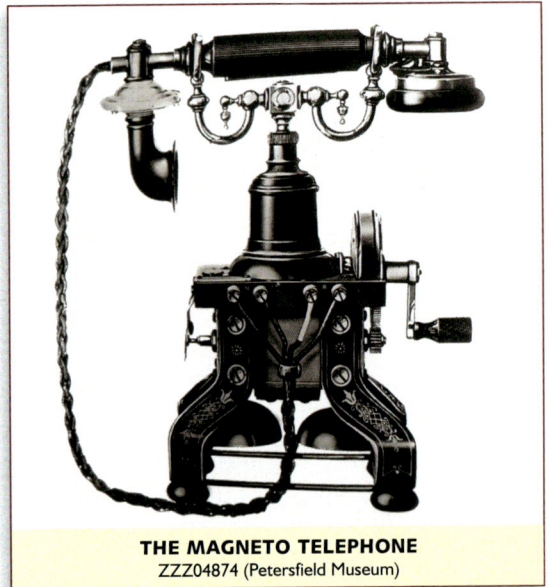

THE FIRST TELEPHONE EXCHANGE
ZZZ04873 (Petersfield Museum)

By the 1920s, telephones had been part of the townscape for a good number of years. The first telephone exchange was behind the building now occupied by estate agents Your Move, and in photograph ZZZ04873, above, the large pole with wires radiating outwards indicates the position of the exchange.

On 10 January 1908 a new exchange (using the magneto system) was installed on the top floor of the post office building, which had been erected in 1892 on a site now occupied by Dolphin Court. 30 years later, on

23 March 1922, another new post office opened in the position it now occupies in the Square, and on 14 February 1928 a new exchange (using the central battery system) was opened here on the top two floors.

For 38 years this exchange served Petersfield, employing more telephone operators as time went by. But technology moves on, and in April 1966 the automatic dial telephone came to Petersfield, together with the modern wonder, Subscriber Trunk Dialling, which was housed in a purpose-built exchange in Charles Street. A further 23 years were to pass until in January 1989 the digital technology telephone came to Petersfield, and with it the telephone system as we know it today.

We must now retrace the progress of the town to the 1930s, when the decision was taken to build a town hall, which had been so sadly lacking for the first 40 years of the Urban District Council's life. Little did the

THE OLD POST OFFICE, HIGH STREET 1898 41319x

THE POST OFFICE 2005 P48736k (Kenneth Hick)

PETERSFIELD'S CREST ZZZ04877
(Petersfield Town Council)

Petersfield's crest is incorporated into the Town Hall floor.

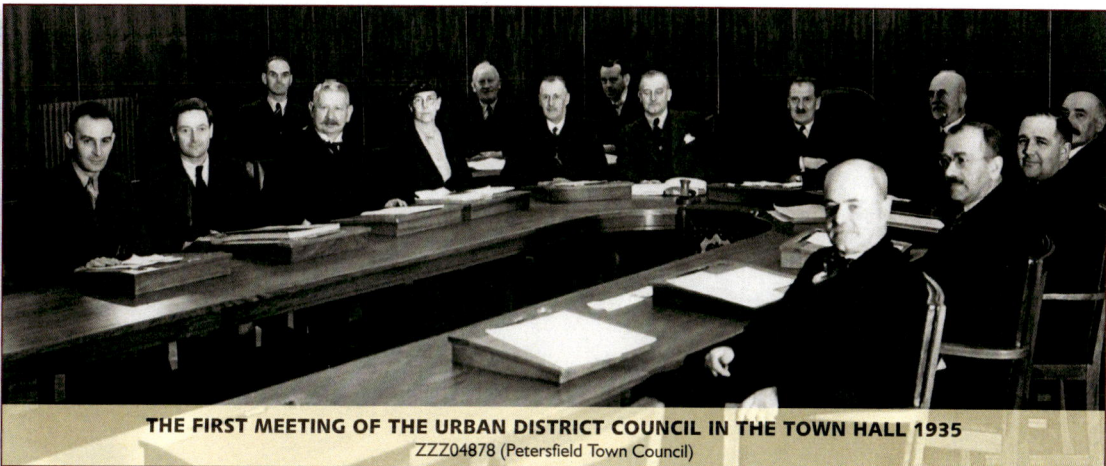

THE FIRST MEETING OF THE URBAN DISTRICT COUNCIL IN THE TOWN HALL 1935
ZZZ04878 (Petersfield Town Council)

ALAN JOHN RAY

Alan was as large a benefactor as the town has ever known. Well-remembered as the Director of Gammon & Smith Ltd, builders' merchants, he took the firm forward to become a national organisation. He was recognised by his peers, and elected president of the Institute of Builders' Merchants in 1977. He was also appointed a Freeman of the City of London. Very much involved in the early 1960s effort to raise finance for Petersfield outdoor swimming pool, he also became the driving force behind the building of the Petersfield Girl Guide Headquarters in the early 70s. He was also chairman of the Board of Governors of the Petersfield School. He was active in the Urban District Council, being its last chairman, and incidentally the first Town Mayor of the Town Council formed in 1974. He strongly promoted the Town Council's desire to provide playing fields, taking the town into the 21st century. Petersfield owes the present Penns Farm playing fields to Alan Ray. St Peter's Church also benefited from his leadership qualities when finance had to be found for the restoration of the organ and for the extensive roof repairs. He recognised the important part played by music in the life of Petersfield, and was a hands-on president of the nationally recognised Petersfield Musical Festival, developing the shape of the festival as it is today. He always said that to be amateur did not mean second-rate! It was as an enlightened and Christian employer with a wry and ready wit that he will be best remembered. He would find a spot for anyone who fell on hard times with the words 'I don't see how Gammon & Smith can continue to exist without you on the staff.'

ALAN JOHN RAY ZZZ04875
(Courtesy of Mary Ray)

GAMMON & SMITH, SWAN STREET 1936
ZZZ04876 (Petersfield Museum)

Not only did the hall, or as it is now known, the Festival Hall, provide for dances, but with such a multi-purpose venue, musical societies and dramatic societies flourished. The first to appear was the Operatic Society in 1936, and after the war in 1948 the Winton Players staged their first performance. The next dramatic society to be formed was the Lion and Unicorn Players in 1959, and in 1968 the Petersfield Hi-Lights gave their first performance on the Festival Hall stage. It was the Hi-Lights that founded the youth theatre venture which has now become an independent organisation known today as the Petersfield Youth Theatre.

A CORNER OF THE MARKET SQUARE c1955
P48008x

councillors realise that within four years of the opening of the Town Hall and its large entertainment hall that the Second World War would mean that there would be a huge demand for all its facilities, particularly for the entertainment of the large number of troops stationed around the town. ABC dances in the hall would attract as many as 500 dancers, with queues for admission. The town had a first-rate facility, and the Urban District Council was very proud of it. The late 1930s style in which it is built may eventually lead to its listing as a building of architectural interest.

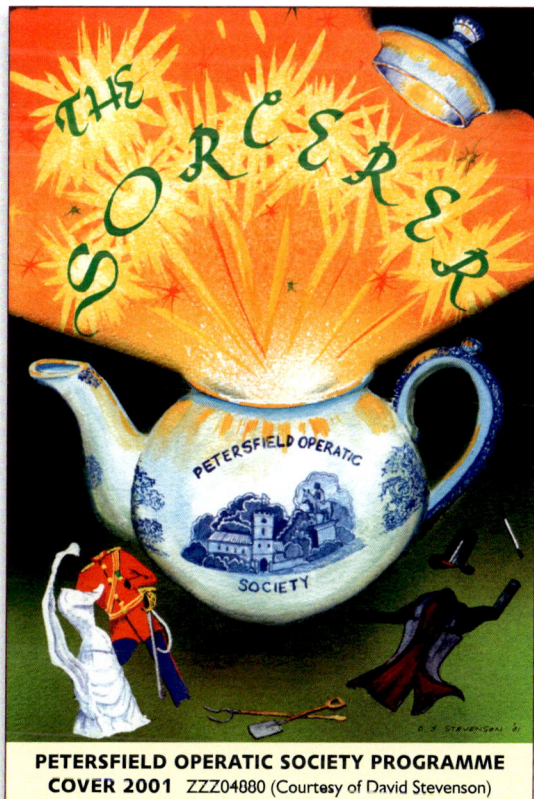

PETERSFIELD OPERATIC SOCIETY PROGRAMME COVER 2001 ZZZ04880 (Courtesy of David Stevenson)

JOHN THOMAS

J T, as he was known, was Engineer and Surveyor to the Petersfield Urban District Council, and after the reorganisation of local government in 1974, deputy engineer to East Hampshire District Council. Brought up in Appledore, North Devon, he never lost his Devon burr. During the Second World War he served with the Royal Engineers in Egypt's western desert. His claim to fame was that following capture, he was put forward to voice the concerns of British PoW's to none other than General Erwin Rommel, commander of the German Africa Corps. When he told the general that

JOHN THOMAS ZZZ04879
(Photographed by the late W A Voice)

the water ration given to the Tommies was meagre, Rommel replied, 'It's no less than my soldiers get.' As John used to say, 'I didn't have an answer to that!' After being a prisoner of war in Poland and Silesia he took part in the infamous forced marches away from the advancing Russians during February and March of 1945. He hardly ever spoke of them and their toll on the men making those long marches, which eventually led to their freedom. He completed his engineering studies after the war, and in 1948 became assistant surveyor to H Longbottom FRICS MIMunE. At that time, shortly after the war, which bankrupted the country, house building was restricted owing to the lack of bricks and other materials. All available resources were put into municipal housing, and licences to build were few and far between. John was given the challenging task of planning and building Grange and Cranford Roads and the Borough Grove development. With the retirement of H Longbottom in 1953, John Thomas took over the role that he so successfully filled of Urban District Council Engineer and Surveyor. At first he ran the town's water supply, as well as sewage disposal, most of the highway maintenance and construction, and also the Heath and the recreation grounds. He was a wise man, particularly with regard to the operation of the Heath and its pond. John was a man of many talents. He was very knowledgeable about the town and its history. He also produced oil paintings of the town, which are cherished to this day by their owners. He left a legacy to Petersfield of four particular buildings, the most important of which is Weston House in Borough Road, one of the first purpose-built sheltered housing units in the country for people of retirement age. It is now planned to demolish the building. His other developments are Petersfield Open Air Swimming Pool and its ancillary buildings, the Central Car Park Toilets, his own house in Woodbury Avenue, and houses in Buckmore Avenue and Sussex Road. The debt of Petersfield to John Thomas C Eng MICE AMIWE in those austere years after the war should never be forgotten.

HIGH STREET c1965 P48078x

Left to right: A medieval building stands beside one from 1934, which is next to one redeveloped in 1955.

Petersfield now has both open-air and enclosed swimming pools, together with a sports centre which is named after the town's annual Taro Fair. The fair, which is of ancient origin and held annually on the weekday nearest to 6 October, brings revellers from many miles to enjoy the fun. It is a fact that there are very few things that you cannot do in Petersfield - it is a place with something for everyone. The only activity not provided for would appear to be Morris dancing.

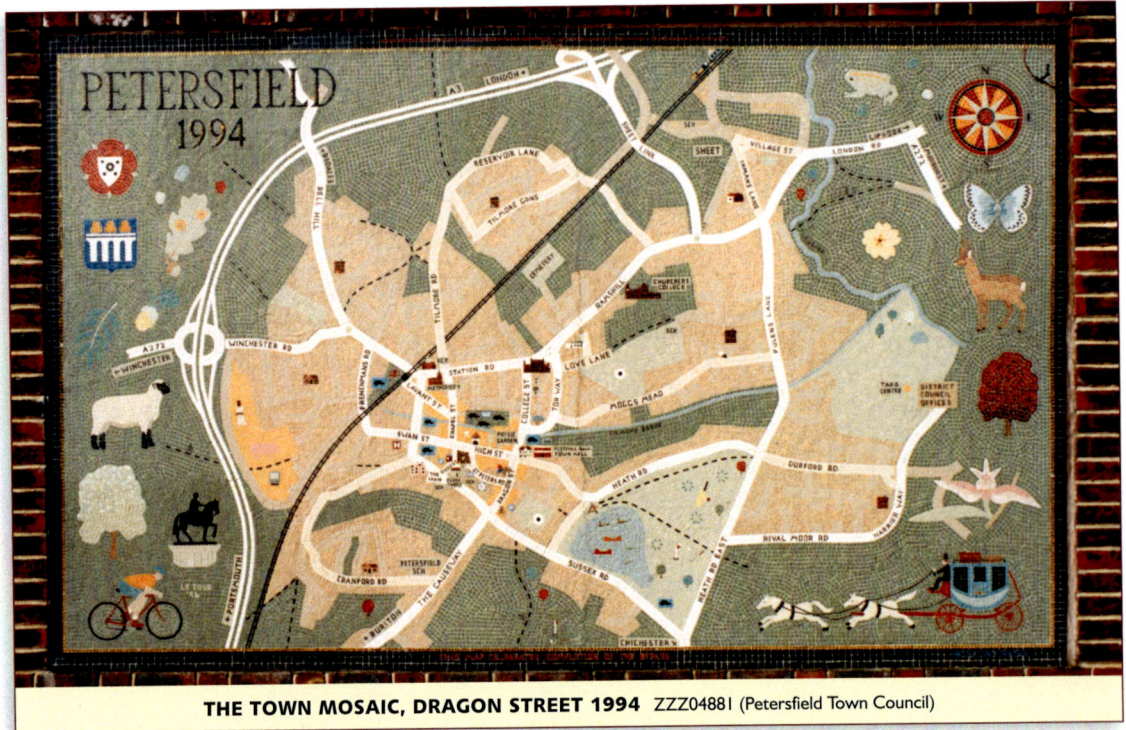

THE TOWN MOSAIC, DRAGON STREET 1994 ZZZ04881 (Petersfield Town Council)

The mosaic commemorates the opening of the 1992 by-pass. This had been eagerly awaited following many years of negotiation and active campaigning. Petersfield would not be the town that it is today without the relief from traffic afforded by its construction.

As to the future, Petersfield has recently been surprised by the announcement that housing in the town will in future be slowed down from the accustomed allowance for a gradual increase in population. A report has recently been received which virtually rules out greenfield development for the town in the near future. This, combined with Petersfield's inclusion in the South Downs National Park, ensures that it will remain a desirable place in which to live and bring up a family. This may augur well for the future; but it will lead to more pressure for redevelopment of existing sites within the town boundary, putting a strain on existing roads, water supplies and other services in a concentrated area. Certainly the provision of affordable housing could cause increasing concern as house prices increase at a higher rate than elsewhere owing to the scarcity of development land.

With an estimated present population of 13,650, Petersfield is justly described as a small market town, but it has the feel of a large village. It is a friendly place, where shopping becomes a social event, as is witnessed by the number of conversations that can be observed during a short walk down the High Street and into the market on Saturday or Wednesday mornings.

THE OLD DRAYTON HOTEL AWAITS ITS FATE
2005 P48737k (Kenneth Hick)

This was laterly a milk depot.

At the moment Petersfield has an interesting mix of housing, as we can see from the number of houses in each council tax band (March 2005). In Band A there are 591 houses, in Band B 680, in Band C 1648, in Band D 1073, in Band E 956, in Band F 653, in Band G 466, and in Band H 7. The total number of houses is 6074. (The author is grateful to the council tax department of East Hampshire District Council for the above figures).

The town has always been a natural focus of activity and entertainment for people from the surrounding villages. One problem facing Petersfield is the need to keep Council Tax to a reasonable level whilst at the same time maintaining the facilities provided not only for the benefit of those who live in the town itself, but in the wider surrounding area. The

THE FARMERS' MARKET 2005 ZZZ04844 (Kenneth Hick)

cost of providing flowers in the town, the maintenance of the Festival Hall, the upkeep of the Heath, contributions towards the outdoor swimming pool, and youth and other facilities, falls to the 6,000 taxpayers of Petersfield. Recently the residents of Sheet have made it known that they want to have their own parish council, another factor which could ultimately affect the income of Petersfield Town Council.

The recently established Business Park on the western outskirts of the town has brought high-tech industry to Petersfield, and with it an influx of skilled labour. Nevertheless, an early morning visit to the railway station will confirm the exodus of workers to London and elsewhere, making Petersfield a net exporter of labour.

Petersfield's position in the new South Downs National Park, when it is created, will not affect its situation within the East Hampshire Area of Outstanding Natural Beauty. The town will continue to be an attractive place to live and in which to do business. Those who live and work here will be very fortunate.

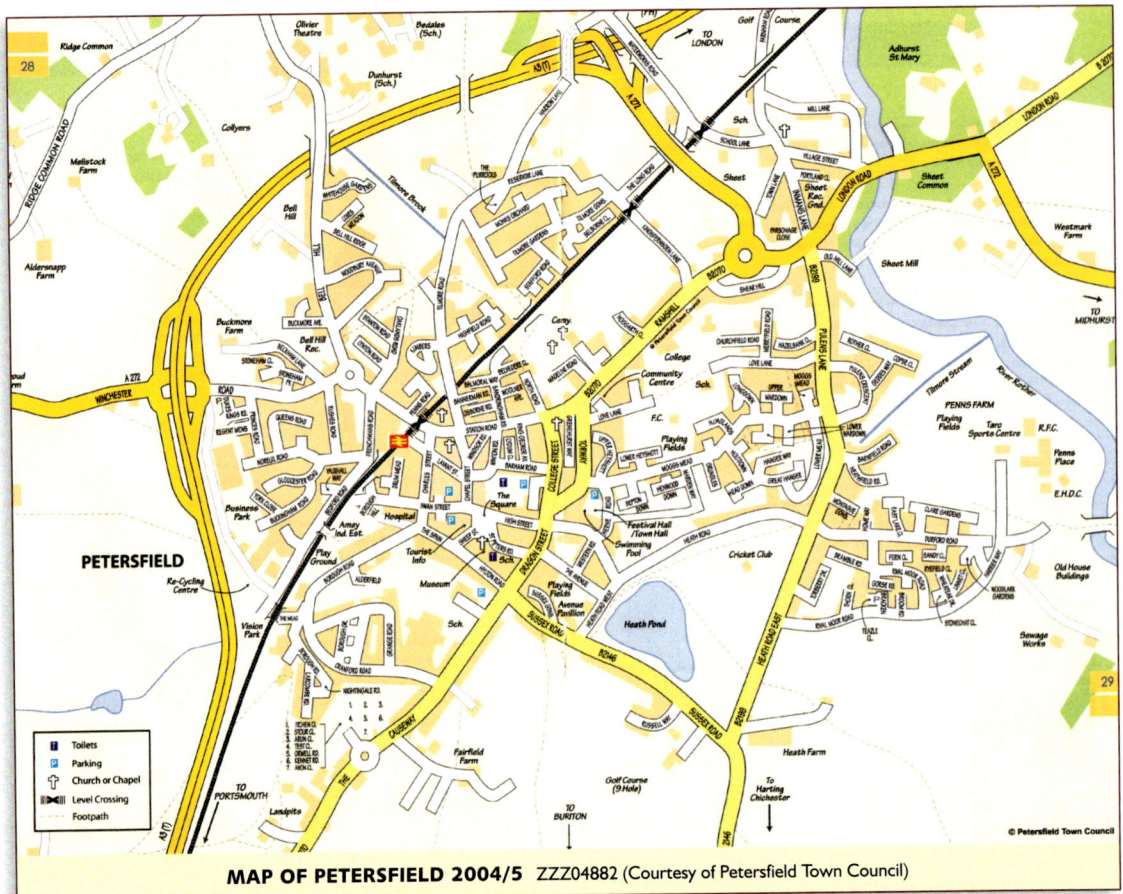

MAP OF PETERSFIELD 2004/5 ZZZ04882 (Courtesy of Petersfield Town Council)

ACKNOWLEDGEMENTS AND BIBLIOGRAPHY

ACKNOWLEDGEMENTS

Mary Ray; Petersfield Museum; Petersfield Town Council; Peter Redman; Roger Hill; David Stevenson; Derek Leach; Ballard's Brewery; Roy Kersley; Jean, my wife; Petersfield Library staff; Natasha Wakefield, Goodwood Collection; The Petersfield Bookshop; Colin Langrish; Peter Greinke; Ann Pinhey.

FURTHER READING LIST:

Petersfield Town Guides, Petersfield Town Council

Petersfield Papers, Petersfield Area Historical Society

Petersfield - A Pictorial Past, Sean Street

Voices of Petersfield, Pamela Payne

Petersfield at War, David Jeffrey

Petersfield Then and Now, Kenneth Hick

A History of Hampshire, Barbara Carpenter-Turner

FRITH PRODUCTS & SERVICES

Francis Frith would doubtless be pleased to know that the pioneering publishing venture he started in 1860 still continues today. Over a hundred and forty years later, The Francis Frith Collection continues in the same innovative tradition and is now one of the foremost publishers of vintage photographs in the world. Some of the current activities include:

INTERIOR DECORATION

Today Frith's photographs can be seen framed and as giant wall murals in thousands of pubs, restaurants, hotels, banks, retail stores and other public buildings throughout the country. In every case they enhance the unique local atmosphere of the places they depict and provide reminders of gentler days in an increasingly busy and frenetic world.

PRODUCT PROMOTIONS

Frith products are used by many major companies to promote the sales of their own products or to reinforce their own history and heritage. Frith promotions have been used by Hovis bread, Courage beers, Scots Porage Oats, Colman's mustard, Cadbury's foods, Mellow Birds coffee, Dunhill pipe tobacco, Guinness, and Bulmer's Cider.

GENEALOGY AND FAMILY HISTORY

As the interest in family history and roots grows world-wide, more and more people are turning to Frith's photographs of Great Britain for images of the towns, villages and streets where their ancestors lived; and, of course, photographs of the churches and chapels where their ancestors were christened, married and buried are an essential part of every genealogy tree and family album.

FRITH PRODUCTS

All Frith photographs are available Framed or just as Mounted Prints and unmounted versions. These may be ordered from the address below. Other products available are - Calendars, Jigsaws, Canvas Prints, Mugs, Tea Towels, Tableware and local and prestige books.

THE INTERNET

Over several hundred thousand Frith photographs can be viewed and purchased on the internet through the Frith websites!

For more detailed information on Frith products, look at
www.francisfrith.com

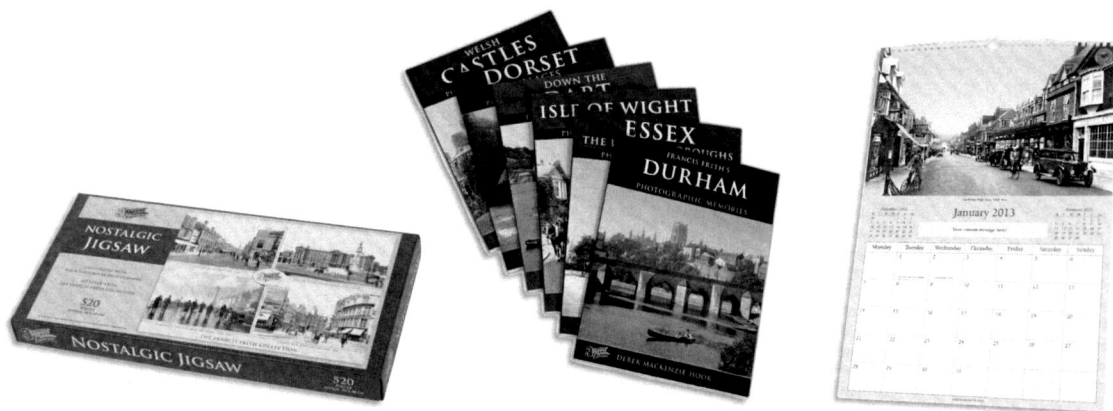

See the complete list of Frith Books at: www.francisfrith.com
This web site is regularly updated with the latest list of publications from The Francis Frith Collection. If you wish to buy books relating to another part of the country that your local bookshop does not stock, you may purchase on-line.

For further information, trade, or author enquiries please contact us at the address below:
The Francis Frith Collection, Unit 19 Kingsmead Business Park, Gillingham, Dorset SP8 5FB.
Tel: +44 (0)1722 716 376   Email: sales@francisfrith.co.uk

See Frith products on the internet at www.francisfrith.com

FREE PRINT OF YOUR CHOICE
CHOOSE A PHOTOGRAPH FROM THIS BOOK

+ POSTAGE

Mounted Print
Overall size 14 x 11 inches (355 x 280mm)

TO RECEIVE YOUR FREE PRINT

Choose any Frith photograph in this book

Simply complete the Voucher opposite and return it with your payment (to cover postage and handling) and we will print the photograph of your choice in SEPIA (size 11 x 8 inches) and supply it in a cream mount ready to frame (overall size 14 x 11 inches).

Order additional Mounted Prints at HALF PRICE - £19.00 each (normally £38.00)

If you would like to order more Frith prints from this book, possibly as gifts for friends and family, you can buy them at half price (with no additional postage costs).

Have your Mounted Prints framed

For an extra £20.00 per print you can have your mounted print(s) framed in an elegant polished wood and gilt moulding, overall size 16 x 13 inches (no additional postage required).

IMPORTANT!

❶ Please note: aerial photographs and photographs with a reference number starting with a "Z" are not Frith photographs and cannot be supplied under this offer.

❷ Offer valid for delivery to one UK address only.

❸ These special prices are only available if you use this form to order. You must use the ORIGINAL VOUCHER on this page (no copies permitted). We can only despatch to one UK address.

❹ This offer cannot be combined with any other offer.

As a customer your name & address will be stored by Frith but not sold or rented to third parties. Your data will be used for the purpose of this promotion only.

Send completed Voucher form to:

**The Francis Frith Collection,
19 Kingsmead Business Park, Gillingham,
Dorset SP8 5FB**

Voucher for **FREE** and Reduced Price *Frith Prints*

Please do not photocopy this voucher. Only the original is valid, so please fill it in, cut it out and return it to us with your order.

Picture ref no	Page no	Qty	Mounted @ £19.00	Framed + £20.00	Total Cost £
		1	Free of charge*	£	£
			£19.00	£	£
			£19.00	£	£
			£19.00	£	£
			£19.00	£	£
			£19.00	£	£

Please allow 28 days for delivery. Offer available to one UK address only

* Post & handling		£3.80
Total Order Cost		£

Title of this book . . . .

I enclose a cheque/postal order for £ . . . . made payable to 'The Francis Frith Collection'

OR please debit my Mastercard / Visa / Maestro card, details below

Card Number:

Issue No (Maestro only):   Valid from (Maestro):

Card Security Number: Expires:

Signature:

Name Mr/Mrs/Ms ....

Address ....

....

....

.... Postcode ....

Daytime Tel No ....

Email ....

Valid to 31/12/20

Free Print – see overleaf

Can you help us with information about any of the Frith photographs in this book?

We are gradually compiling an historical record for each of the photographs in the Frith archive. It is always fascinating to find out the names of the people shown in the pictures, as well as insights into the shops, buildings and other features depicted.

If you recognize anyone in the photographs in this book, or if you have information not already included in the author's caption, do let us know. We would love to hear from you, and will try to publish it in future books or articles.

An Invitation from The Francis Frith Collection to Share Your Memories

The 'Share Your Memories' feature of our website allows members of the public to add personal memories relating to the places featured in our photographs, or comment on others already added. Seeing a place from your past can rekindle forgotten or long held memories. Why not visit the website, find photographs of places you know well and add YOUR story for others to read and enjoy? We would love to hear from you!

www.francisfrith.com/memories

Our production team

Frith books are produced by a small dedicated team at offices near Salisbury. Most have worked with the Frith Collection for many years. All have in common one quality: they have a passion for the Frith Collection.

Frith Books and Gifts

We have a wide range of books and gifts available on our website utilising our photographic archive, many of which can be individually personalised.

www.francisfrith.com

FF025700